T0322067

LIVE FREE EAT WELL

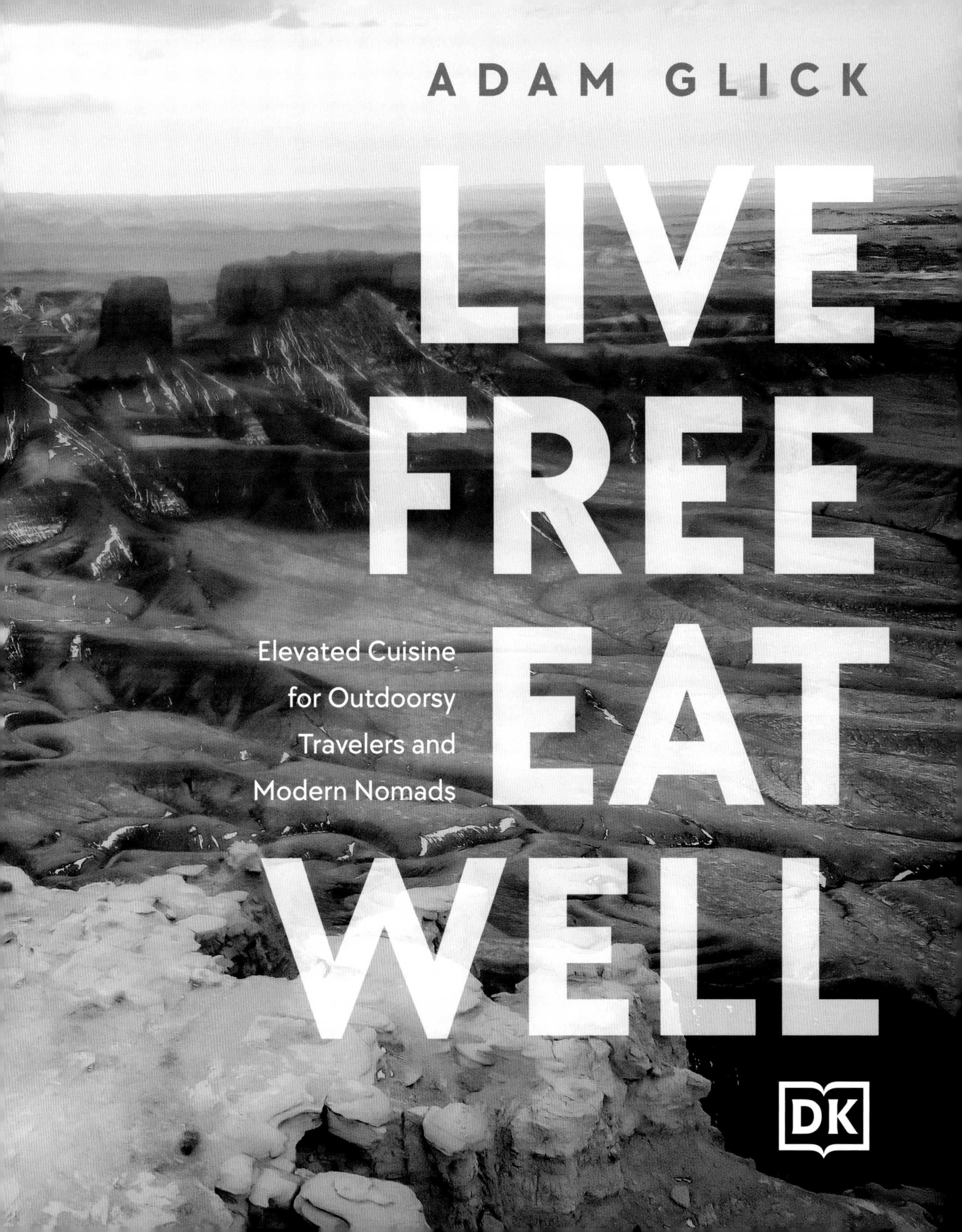

ADAM GLICK

LIVE FREE EAT WELL

Elevated Cuisine
for Outdoorsy
Travelers and
Modern Nomads

DK

Publisher Mike Sanders
Senior Editor Alexander Rigby
Editorial Director Ann Barton
Art & Design Director William Thomas
Assistant Director of Art & Design Rebecca Batchelor
Photographer Adam Glick
Illustrator Claire Loon Baldwin
Recipe Tester Robert Naugle III
Copy Editor Devon Fredericksen
Proofreaders Claire Safran, Amy Schneider
Indexer Celia McCoy

First American Edition, 2024
Published in the United States by DK Publishing
1745 Broadway, 20th Floor, New York, NY 10019

The authorized representative in the EEA is Dorling Kindersley
Verlag GmbH. Arnulfstr. 124, 80636 Munich, Germany

Copyright © 2024 by Adam Glick
DK, a Division of Penguin Random House LLC
24 25 26 27 28 10 9 8 7 6 5 4 3 2
002-341124-JUN2024

All rights reserved.
Without limiting the rights under the copyright reserved
above, no part of this publication may be reproduced, stored
in or introduced into a retrieval system, or transmitted, in any
form, or by any means (electronic, mechanical, photocopying,
recording, or otherwise), without the prior written permission
of the copyright owner.

Library of Congress Number: 2023947875
ISBN 978-0-7440-9945-4

DK books are available at special discounts when purchased
in bulk for sales promotions, premiums, fund-raising, or
educational use. For details, contact SpecialSales@dk.com

Printed and bound in Italy

www.dk.com

This book was made with Forest
Stewardship Council™ certified
paper – one small step in DK's
commitment to a sustainable future.
Learn more at
www.dk.com/uk/information/sustainability

For the love of freedom.

For taking the road less traveled.

And for those who have followed my journey.

Without you, none of this is possible. Thank you.

CONTENTS

CONTENTS BY MEAL

DINNER

DESSERT

EXTRAS

INTRODUCTION

Living free and eating well is a way to cook differently. It's a style of cooking I've adopted after spending years preparing food in tiny spaces. The goal of this type of food preparation is not only to feed yourself and others but to use minimal ingredients and equipment, and lots of intuition any time you're making a new dish. This is a cookbook that encourages you to think beyond just these recipes' steps and ingredients. I hope you'll take the lessons and techniques shared here and apply them to future recipes of your own. Written recipes are meant to serve as a guide, in my opinion. A lack of creativity is the only thing keeping you from turning water into wine. Work with what you have, don't be afraid to bend the rules a bit, and try to create your own unique version of the dish every time. I want to encourage you to think outside the box, and attempt new, maybe even unconventional techniques, when preparing food in tight spaces or unusual places. By using methods that create less mess and avoid clutter, you'll be able to enjoy the experience of cooking more fully.

My style of cooking could best be described as "working with what you have." I believe this leads to endless possibilities and boundless creativity. I'm sure most people can relate to this, since making special trips to the grocery store or not having what you need can often be a limiting factor whenever you're trying to cook something new. In my culinary world, not having what I need is expected, as I'm always on the go, seeing new places, and setting up different rigs. It's knowing how to overcome any situation that might make cooking outdoors or in a tight space less intuitive. When you understand how to consolidate your cooking methods by using less equipment and fewer ingredients, you ultimately save yourself time and effort. I learned these techniques from the years I spent cooking at sea, in an environment that is not always friendly to chefs. Making meals in tight spaces, on moving vessels, in new locations, with unknown provisions, on rough seas, and during cross-country road trips in various rigs hasn't always been easy, to say the least. Most chefs tend to work in a standard, stable kitchen, and somehow, I avoided that.

With this cookbook, my goal is to impart some of the wisdom I've gained during my time using this less-than-conventional style of cooking, which ended up making my life a little bit easier, if you can believe it. The beautiful thing is, these techniques and lessons don't just apply to how I cook on the go; they're equally useful in everyday cookery at home, at sea, or on a long road trip. My experiences have molded me into a certain type of chef, and I have long wanted to create a cookbook centered on this alternative lifestyle.

Above all else, I hope you'll use this book to try out new things, both with food and in life. If I use a certain ingredient in a recipe, don't feel like you absolutely have to use it. Feel free to switch it up, use what's in season, or add what you already have. Don't feel restricted by these recipes. I want this cookbook to serve as a guide to teach you new things about cooking. If you can learn how to cook and master the basic principles that make food taste good, then you can apply these skills to any ingredient or combination of recipe steps.

This cookbook has given me the opportunity to show you how I like to cook, to share my photography, to tell stories from my travels, and to maybe inspire others to live free and eat well. Thanks for coming on this journey with me.

MY STORY

I was always destined to travel. From the day I was born, the adventure began. Before I graduated high school, my sister, parents, and I had lived on three different continents. From attending elementary school in Central Africa to evacuating from Kuwait City during 9/11 in high school, I've had many life experiences that've broadened my perspective. Being exposed to different cultures and belief systems and a multitude of cuisines instilled in me a love for adventure. I didn't know it then, but all this traveling when I was young prepared me for what would become a lifetime of exploring the world.

After high school, I went to college in Northern California. I only lasted two years studying graphic design, since I didn't particularly enjoy being a college student. Sitting in a classroom regurgitating information just wasn't for me. I needed to learn with my hands and be able to touch, feel, and experiment to enjoy learning. My sister picked up on this and suggested I go to culinary school. I didn't have a penny to my name at the time, but I spent what little money I did have on ingredients from the local bargain food store to cook meals and experiment making dishes for my friends and family. Eventually, I heeded my sister's advice and dropped out of college and enrolled in culinary school.

While learning how to cook, I bounced around from restaurant to restaurant trying to find my place in the cuisine world. At one point, I found myself in a San Diego hotel surrounded by fifty-pound bags of potatoes that I was tasked with peeling. I knew I had the skills and creativity to do better, to do more. So that's why I'll never forget the day an email came through offering me my first job on a boat, which ultimately changed my life forever. I quit my job at the hotel that same day, not even having interviewed yet. I had nothing but hope and a poorly written résumé. Jobless, I interviewed, and within a week I was flying to Alaska to get on my first boat. Packing everything up and taking this risk

wasn't anything new to me. In fact, it felt almost normal, since it was so similar to my experiences traveling as a child. This was the beginning of what would become more than a decade of cooking on the high seas, sailing more than 100,000 nautical miles from Australia to Greece and everywhere else in between.

Visiting new places by water was unlike any other method of travel I had experienced previously. I was forced to familiarize myself with new towns, cultures, and languages in a matter of hours to quickly find all the necessities for the next leg of the journey. Gathering specific foods, supplies, and other items in a foreign place was no easy task when I didn't speak the language or have an iPhone to google where the local farmers market was. Yet over the years, I found that these ocean-based communities have some of the most welcoming, friendly, and accepting people in the world. I'm forever grateful to have been able to see the world this way because it helped me shape my own understanding of what it means to live free and eat well.

After ten successful years of yachting, I found myself on a yacht in Alaska tasked with cooking for my largest number of guests yet. I was cooking for not one, but two super yachts simultaneously. Side by side, we traveled among the icebergs through Alaskan waters. One day, I was requested to make warm cookies for the other vessel. I hopped to, made a fresh batch of warm chocolate chip cookies, loaded them onto the tender (the boat used to supply provisions between ships), and ferried the cookies through a minefield of icebergs to the other yacht. Unfortunately for me, the cookies were sent back because they were deemed not warm enough. In the final hours of this charter, with my head in my hands, I stood on the top deck that overlooked the two yachts filled with guests and wondered how much more of this I had left in me.

As fate would have it, I shortly received yet another email that would change my life. During my yachting career, I had a brief appearance on the Food Network in a competition cooking show. Contacts from that agency had been following my career and were working on a series called *Below Deck*. They'd reached out to me before to ask me to cook on this new show that was based in Europe. I had initially declined their offers out of fear that being on the show would ruin my culinary career. But on this day, on that top deck in Alaska, I received their final offer to be the next chef on *Below Deck*. I figured there was no way a TV show could put me through what I'd just been through on this grueling two-week charter. So without hesitation, I responded, "Yes. I'm ready." My formal yachting career had begun in Alaska and so it ended there, too.

From that day forward, my career as a chef was in the public eye. Overnight, I went from having complete solace in a galley to being surrounded by network cameras and microphones at all hours of the day, seven days a week. If I thought the warm cookies were as annoying as it could get, I was wrong. I appeared in three seasons of *Below Deck* over the span of five years, entertaining the world with my no-nonsense attitude and culinary antics. My new life on camera led to me having a popular social media presence, which allowed me to explore teaching my fans how to cook. Coming from a long line of teachers, it felt natural to share the expertise I'd gained over years of being in a galley with this new platform. My time spent on network television propelled me into what became the next chapter of my life: inspiring people through my love of cooking via the power of social media.

After a lifetime of incessant travel and experiencing the world by way of water, I felt it was time to explore by way of land. Now in my late thirties, I'm learning how to plant roots for the first time, even though I know I will always have the travel bug. During my yachting career it was an open secret that I spent my off days in a live-aboard vehicle, so I was already accustomed to what I like to call "land

yachts." I've found that the perfect balance for me at this stage in my life is having a home-base cabin in the Pacific Northwest and a truck camper capable of taking me and my dog, Tex, anywhere I desire. I can have all the comforts of having a home, while still maintaining the ability to escape in my truck on any adventure at the drop of a hat.

In a way, I've always had the option of leaving port (my home) and going out to sea (the highway). So in that way, my career as a traveling adventure chef never really ended, it merely transformed to better fit the lifestyle I wanted for myself. I found a way to feed people that makes me happy, while also reinvigorating my love for cooking. No more fancy five-star plates for billionaires. I only want to cook in a way that feels authentic to me and aligns with my lifestyle and values with my newfound land-based life. Using my love for the outdoors to stay connected with people and food allows me to continue a professional career as a chef and to do what I love, all while feeding people by cooking over a well-built fire.

I've always embodied a sense of independence, ever since I was young. It continued in my professional career as a chef, and today I feel as though I can't do anything besides remain free— free to make my own decisions, free to make changes when necessary, and free to experience life to the fullest. The decisions I've made, though questionable at times, have been nothing but a whirlwind of new experiences and life lessons. I wouldn't take them back for the world.

Over the years I've tended to work solo. Just about everything I do, I do by myself. I don't have an agent or team of people helping me. There's no social media manager or content creator behind the scenes. There are no professional photographers following me around, or food stylists making sure everything is perfect. The words and photos in this book represent me because I created all of it. When I reflect on how the odds were stacked against me after my time on television, I'm proud to say I've achieved a lot all on my own. It was through my hard work and perseverance that my dreams became a reality.

HOW TO USE THIS BOOK

This book is written a bit differently than your typical cookbook. I seem to enjoy making everything different from what it's "supposed" to be. There are no chapters specifically designated for appetizers, soups, entrées, or desserts. Instead, every chapter is a lesson, leading you to discover a new way of thinking about food and cooking. The objective with every recipe in this book is to teach you that it's not about where you cook or what you cook with, it's how you do it. You can be on top of a mountain by a fire, on a boat, in a camper, or in your home kitchen, and all the principles I explain in this cookbook still apply. My hope is that you'll make your way through each chapter and come out with a new way of cooking that you've never tried before.

We begin with *The Basics*, a general introduction to some of the cooking techniques that will be used most frequently throughout the book. Master these techniques and you'll be off to a great start. As we go through the chapters, I'll ease you into different styles and ways of cooking. I'll show you how to *Be Prepared* when making a dish and how to ensure that you always have the right *Equipment* at your disposal. These two chapters will teach you important lessons about gathering only the necessities for preparing beautiful dishes, anywhere.

We'll travel through my life cooking *On the Road* and *On the Water*, showcasing the lessons I learned through a career of making food while traveling. The skills needed to make successful dishes *Over a Fire* will be shared, as will the secrets of *One-Pot Cookery*. Finally, I'll share the ways you can effectively prepare food *In a Small Space*, how to take advantage of *Cross-Utilization* for your recipes, and what *Less Is More* really means.

Every one of these chapters contains recipes from appetizers to desserts and every other kind of dish you could want. To find a particular type of food you'd like to make, you can quickly reference the contents by meal list at the start of the book.

The techniques used when cooking are what matter most. Don't fixate only on what to cook tonight—flipping to that recipe, making the dish, and then forgetting the lessons learned. I set out to create a cookbook that encourages you to absorb this book as a whole, mastering the techniques that define each recipe. By creating a cookbook with a less traditional structure, I believe I can share wisdom from my time as a chef and also help you learn as we go.

If you're seeking vegan or gluten-free recipes, look out for the ⓥ or ⓖⓕ icons at the top of the recipe page. These icons indicate that the recipe follows these dietary restrictions.

LIVE FREE, EAT WELL

Humans are nomadic at heart. In the past, we moved when the food moved. The modern world has changed all that, though, and now we're used to eating strawberries in the middle of winter. These days, we often forget what it takes to create a strawberry in the first place and the joy that comes from indulging in the fruits of our labor. We can indulge in delicious fruits year-round, even though nature intended these delectable morsels to shine for just a select couple of months each year. Today, our local grocery store provides us these delights at the flip of a switch, which has reduced our appreciation for what it means to source quality ingredients during the appropriate season. When things get too easy, we get complacent. Fast forward, and microwaves and Instant Pots have replaced the need to hone an array of cooking skills. As a result, the traditions and techniques that worked flawlessly for hundreds of years are being forgotten.

Our knowledge of what good food is, where it comes from, and how to prepare it is dwindling. In addition, our understanding that food should be seasonal, local, and cherished at a specific time of year has been all but forgotten. For certain fruits, you used to have to wait all year for a brief period when you could enjoy these perfectly ripe natural treats. Now that we have access to them and other seasonal ingredients all year long, food is almost too easy to come by, and as a result, we often take for granted how easy it is to get food at the grocery store. Ultimately, we don't enjoy these seasonal ingredients as much as we should because we don't stop to consider what had to happen for them to make it into our shopping cart.

Less than a hundred years ago, we would have worked hard just to get a handful of perfectly sun-ripened berries. We certainly wouldn't have let those berries go to waste. Living free and eating well discourages throwing the berries away because you forgot about them and they went bad. Instead, this lifestyle is about making them into a pie or a delicious jam that you can store and enjoy for weeks to come. When we live free and eat well, we can purchase less and use fewer ingredients. We can work with what we have and utilize leftovers to make new dishes. The goal is one hundred percent utilization, being resourceful, and taking only what you need. These practices will lead you down a path that is better for humanity, while also bringing you joy and fulfillment, all while using less. When living a nomadic lifestyle or even when taking a weekend camping trip, we quickly come to understand how less is often more. I've found that some of the best meals I've ever created came from just a few high-quality ingredients. You can make a big fire with little twigs.

When humans stopped traveling and moved into big cities, we lost touch with our nomadic roots. Yet many of us still have a desire to experience what a nomadic lifestyle is like. We yearn to see more of the world around us, to be immersed in nature, to indulge in the fruits it provides, and, most of all, to be more aligned with our nomadic past. My life of travel led me to become the chef I am today, and it was my willingness to get up and go that makes me, and this cookbook, different. I have experienced countless cultures firsthand, come to understand their ways of living, their food, and their cooking techniques. Ultimately, I've discovered how much happier people are when they're living life the way we did for thousands of years. A simple life of sustenance is all we really need.

For most, living in a city is the way of life—eating out, paying for groceries, using fancy kitchen appliances. But what if, instead, we took a road trip, stopped at a farmers market to get fresh produce on the way, and cooked it up somewhere in the great outdoors? Hell, pack up and take a walk to the park if that's all you have access to. The human experience of gathering goods, finding a view, and enjoying a meal in nature is one of the greatest things we can do for ourselves on this earth. But you have to be willing to go. Even if being nomadic isn't your thing, chances are you're itching to experience food in a different way, you just don't know it yet.

THE BASICS

It's the principle of the recipe that matters most, not so much the ingredients. It's bold to insinuate that ingredients don't matter, because of course they do, but not as much as knowing how to cook. A good chef can make a delicious meal with very few ingredients, even low-quality ingredients. They can open the cupboards and fridge, look around, and say, "I've got this." This kind of cook is willing to experiment, be creative, and think outside the box. They cook with a sense of freedom, no longer depending on a cookbook or special runs to the grocery store to make a specific dish.

Many amazing recipes are born out of necessity. When a chef is pressed for ingredients, a few leftover food items and a bit of experimentation can lead to a new recipe. My best advice to the aspiring cook is to look at the recipes you want to make and use them as a guide to learn the basic principles of cookery. Don't just start with the goal to replicate the dish. Find out how the dish was originally made, what techniques help perfect it, and extract these lessons and apply them to the other recipes you want to make in the future, with the goal of eventually creating your own recipes from scratch.

By absorbing various cooking techniques, you open yourself up to the freedom of working with virtually any ingredients available to you. You can mix and match ingredients based on what's already lying around the house and not be hindered by using only the ingredients listed in a recipe. A cook should always be intuitive and flexible. Don't have butter? Use olive oil. Don't have fish? Use chicken. Don't have the right spice? Try another you do have. The willingness to be flexible will change how you cook and how much fun you have doing it. Be open to the idea of failure. Throughout your cooking journey, you will make mistakes. Don't let this get you down. Instead, learn from these mistakes and do your best to make a change to achieve your desired results the next time.

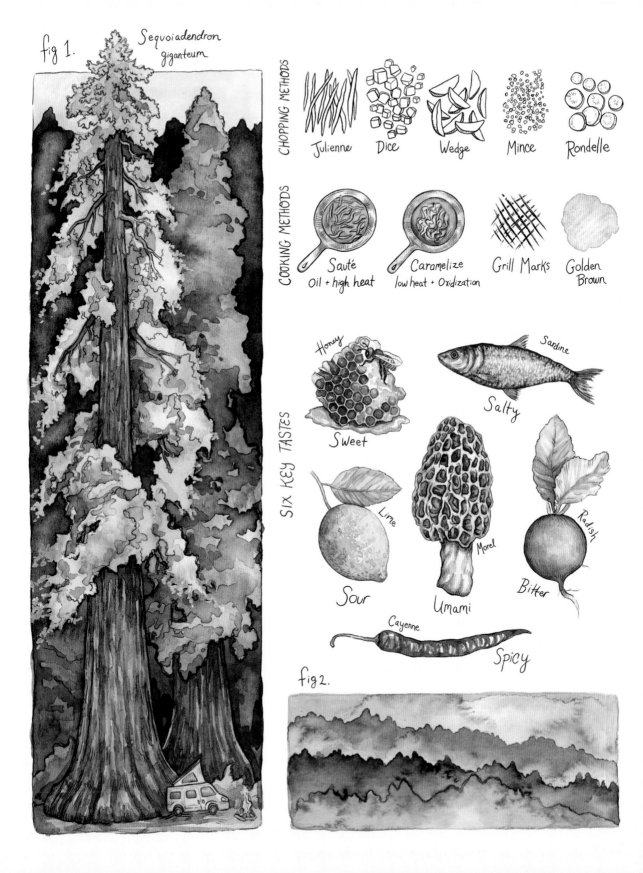

fig 1.

Sequoiadendron giganteum

CHOPPING METHODS

Julienne Dice Wedge Mince Rondelle

COOKING METHODS

Sauté
Oil + high heat

Caramelize
low heat + Oxidization

Grill Marks

Golden Brown

SIX KEY TASTES

Honey
Sweet

Sardine
Salty

Lime
Sour

Morel
Umami

Radish
Bitter

Cayenne
Spicy

fig 2.

This chapter includes recipes that discuss basic techniques to help you succeed as an aspiring adventure chef. Even if you already know how to cook, these recipes are a good reminder of what to focus on: techniques and go-to foundational dishes.

- **Knife skills:** how they can make food taste better and make your life easier in the kitchen

- **Caramelization:** the application of heat to convert natural sugars into big flavors

- **Stirring:** knowing when and how to stir may be basic as can be, but it remains an important cooking skill

- **Application of heat:** it doesn't matter where the heat comes from; it's how you apply it

- **Stocks and broths:** the basis of all great savory cuisine

- **Baking breads:** one of the most satisfying additions to any meal

The fact is, there are too many techniques and go-to foundational recipes to list them all in detail, but the ones in this chapter are a great place to start.

As you embark on the adventure of becoming a better cook, always remember that it doesn't matter where you cook, as long as you understand the techniques and the objectives of the recipe. I was once forced to feed twelve people for an entire month using only a propane grill. Being challenged this way, I learned very quickly how to adapt to my heat source and continue cooking as usual. By understanding the basic principles of cooking, I was able to overcome obstacles to create delicious meals in a less-than-conventional kitchen. I challenge you, similarly, to experiment with food, both at your home and on the road. This will help you become a better chef, while also creating less work that leads to better, tastier results.

MAKES: 2QT (2L) | PREP: 15 MINUTES | COOK: 1–48 HOURS | GF

BONE BROTH

Bone broth is the basis of great cooking. With a homemade bone broth, you can enhance the flavors of dishes like soups, sautéed vegetables, rice, risotto, and stuffing. Anything that can soak up flavor should be soaking up bone broth. It's also a terrific way to use up veggie scraps; nearly anything that can be composted can be made into stock. At home, I keep a pot simmering on the stove, ready to throw in scraps of onion, carrot peels, and the tops and bottoms of celery. The broth on the stove keeps my house warm and filled with a delicious aroma. I will often dip my mug into the pot and sip on a cup of hot broth throughout the day. So, use this as a way to achieve complete utilization. Don't throw away extra scraps. Instead, turn them into liquid gold.

1 whole roasted chicken carcass

1 onion, roughly chopped

2 ribs celery, roughly chopped

2 carrots, roughly chopped

2 bay leaves

1 tbsp salt

1 Begin by preparing your heat source. You'll need a fire or a stovetop burner set at low heat.

2 To a large stockpot, add the chicken carcass, onion, celery, carrots, bay leaves, and salt. Fill the pot ¾ full with water.

3 Place over low heat and bring to a simmer. (Do not allow the broth to boil; this will compromise the clarity.) Simmer uncovered for at least 1 hour for a light broth and up to 48 hours for the fullest possible flavor. Add small amounts of water as needed to keep the bones and vegetables submerged, and periodically skim any foam that forms on the surface.

4 After simmering, strain the broth. Place a mesh sieve or colander over a second large pot or container, and slowly pour the broth through the sieve, removing the bones and vegetable solids. (These can be discarded.)

Broth can be created using just vegetables as well. A broth can be made by extracting the flavor from just about any ingredient. Vegetable stock is great for making risotto, soups, and sautéing vegetables, and is vegetarian friendly.

SERVES: 4 | PREP: 15 MINUTES, PLUS 1 HOUR TO RISE | COOK: 10 MINUTES

GARLIC HERB FLATBREAD

When in the outdoors or when cooking in general, it's helpful to use minimal ingredients that create a big impact. Homemade flatbread is a great example of this principle. This simple recipe is inspired by the flatbread I ate while growing up in the Middle East. With only four basic ingredients, you can create bakery-fresh bread at your campsite or at home. I like to brush it with a garlic-herb butter for even more flavor.

1 tbsp active dry yeast

2½ cups (300g) all-purpose flour

2 tsp salt

8 tbsp butter, melted

2 garlic cloves, minced

5 sprigs parsley, minced

1 In a large bowl, combine the yeast and 1 cup (240ml) warm water. Let sit for 5 minutes, allowing the yeast to bloom.

2 To the bowl with the yeast, add the flour gradually, stirring it in with a wooden spoon. Add the salt. Continue mixing for at least 5 minutes, until the dough starts to pull away from the sides of the bowl. Sprinkle with a little more of the flour if the dough is still wet and sticky.

3 Cover the bowl with a damp towel and let rise in a warm area for 1 hour.

4 Once the dough has risen, lightly dust a large cutting board with flour. Transfer the dough to the cutting board, and divide it into 4 pieces of equal size. Form each portion of dough into a ball, rolling and shaping it between your palms in a circular motion.

5 Let the dough balls rest for 5 minutes. This will allow the dough to relax.

6 While the dough is resting, prepare your heat source. You'll need a fire or a grill preheated to 400°F (200°C). In a small bowl, combine the melted butter, garlic, and parsley. Set aside.

7 Using your hands or a rolling pin, stretch the dough into thin, flat circles. Place directly onto the hot grill. Flip the bread when bubbles appear.

8 Once the bread is crispy and lightly charred, remove from the heat and liberally brush with the garlic butter.

This bread makes a fantastic accompaniment to soups, curries, chili, and dips. Use this bread to make pita pockets, gyros, or even quick little pizzas.

SERVES: 4 | PREP: 5 MINUTES | COOK: 20–30 MINUTES (V) (GF)

CRISPY SWEET POTATO WEDGES

Knowing how to roast or caramelize vegetables is the most important thing to take away from this recipe. If you disrupt your ingredients too much by stirring, pushing, or pulling the items around, you're disrupting the beautiful process of caramelization. When it comes to this recipe, be sure to let it rest. If it seems like the sweet potatoes are starting to burn, move the hot ones to the outside and the outside ones into the hot zone. Typically, the very center of your pan is the hot zone. Be proactive about creating caramelization, and don't move or flip the potatoes until you see they have some color.

2 large sweet potatoes, sliced into long wedges

½ white onion, thinly sliced

3–4 garlic cloves, peeled

4 tbsp olive oil

Salt and pepper, to taste

1 lemon, cut in half, to garnish

1 bunch of oregano, to garnish

1 Begin by preparing your heat source. You'll need a fire or an oven preheated to 400°F (200°C).

2 To a skillet or roasting pan, add the potatoes, onion, and garlic. Be sure they are evenly spaced.

3 Coat the vegetables thoroughly with olive oil, salt, and pepper.

4 If using a skillet over the fire, cook for 20 minutes until golden brown. If using the oven, roast for 30 minutes. When finished, remove from the heat and let cool.

5 Quickly roast the lemon halves directly over your heat source for a few minutes until they are slightly charred.

6 Garnish with fresh oregano and the roasted lemon halves.

The trick here is to not mess with the vegetables as they cook. Don't stir or flip them—just let them be until they're golden brown on one side. Leaving the potato skins on will help keep them together.

SERVES: 5 | PREP: 20 MINUTES | COOK: 1–1½ HOURS GF

POTATOES AU GRATIN

The art of gratin is that you can add an au gratin element to just about anything. While this culinary technique is very similar to the principles used in caramelization, here we are focused on providing heat only to the surface of the food. This is especially the case with this recipe or any other dishes you come across that have a delicious, crunchy, cheesy texture layered on top. The broiling that's needed to perfect this recipe can be done using your pizza oven, regular oven, Dutch oven, or even a torch. As you'll soon learn, broiling and making a dish au gratin will take it to the next level.

Olive oil or butter

½ white onion, thinly sliced

3 medium Russet potatoes, cut into ¼-inch (6-mm) slices

3 cups (300g) freshly grated Gruyère cheese or smoked gouda cheese

6oz (180g) heavy whipping cream

Salt and pepper, to taste

Fresh thyme, to garnish

1 Begin by preparing your heat source. You'll need a fire or an oven preheated to 325°F (160°C).

2 Grease a shallow cast-iron skillet (or any fire-safe medium-sized pan) with olive oil or butter. Be sure to coat the surface thoroughly.

3 In the bottom of the skillet, spread a thin layer of onion, followed by a single layer of potatoes, a layer of ½ cup (50g) of the cheese, and a drizzle of the heavy whipping cream. Season lightly with salt and pepper. Repeat the process until the pan is filled to the top and all ingredients are used.

4 Cover the pan with aluminum foil and cook or bake for 1 to 1½ hours.

5 Check the doneness by sticking a table knife into the center. If the knife touches the bottom of the pan with little resistance, the potatoes are done.

6 Top with more cheese and give the dish a quick broil (if using an oven) or enjoy as is. Serve warm, and garnish with the thyme.

Knowing and understanding the art of broiling will allow you to cook steaks to perfection, keep proteins moist, and add an additional layer of texture to your food.

ROASTED CAULIFLOWER
WITH PARMESAN

Cauliflower can be cooked in a variety of different ways: roasted in the oven, on the grill, over a campfire with a cast-iron skillet, in a pizza oven, or under a broiler. Maintaining an even cooking temperature ensures fewer hot spots, and that's a good thing. Fewer hot spots means you won't have to fuss with the food as much, resulting in an even distribution of caramelization. When making this recipe, I prefer using a cast-iron skillet because it helps keep the heat more evenly dispersed.

1 head cauliflower, cut into florets

½ white onion, thinly sliced

6 garlic cloves, diced

1 tsp salt

½ tsp pepper

2 tbsp olive oil

1 cup (100g) freshly grated Parmesan cheese

Chopped fresh oregano, to garnish

1 Begin by preparing your heat source. You'll need a fire or an oven preheated to 350°F (180°C).

2 In a large bowl, combine the cauliflower, onion, garlic, salt, and pepper. Coat with the olive oil, and mix to ensure that all ingredients are thoroughly covered.

3 Add the mixed ingredients to a skillet or roasting pan, and spread in an even layer. Sprinkle on the grated cheese.

4 If using a skillet over the fire, cook for 20 minutes until golden brown. If using the oven, roast for 25 minutes.

5 Remove the skillet from the heat and garnish with fresh oregano. Serve warm.

It is okay to have both a hot spot and a cool spot, but be aware of where they both are so you can use them to your advantage.

SERVES: 5 | PREP: 20 MINUTES | COOK: 1½ HOURS

SHRIMP CREOLE
WITH POLENTA

When I was growing up, my family often made dishes featuring Louisiana Creole flavors like the ones in this dish. Shrimp and andouille sausage are cooked in a richly seasoned sauce made with the holy trinity—onion, bell pepper, and celery—and served over creamy, cheesy polenta. The beautiful thing about this recipe is how much better it tastes the next day. Bring the prepared shrimp topping with you on your next outing and all you have to make at the site is the polenta. Warm up your shrimp and you have a delicious dinner.

FOR THE POLENTA:

1 cup (160g) yellow polenta

1 tbsp salt

4 tbsp butter

1 cup (120g) grated cheddar cheese

2 cups (350g) corn kernels (cut from 2 ears grilled corn or thawed from frozen)

FOR THE SHRIMP CREOLE:

25 medium shell-on shrimp

2 tbsp ghee (or clarified butter), divided in half

8oz (225g) andouille sausage, diced

4 tbsp Cajun seasoning, divided in half

½ yellow onion, diced

3 garlic cloves, minced

2 ribs celery, diced

1 bell pepper, diced

1 cup (200g) diced tomato

1 tbsp all-purpose flour

Oregano leaves, to garnish

1   Begin by preparing your heat source. You'll need a fire or stovetop burner set at medium-high heat. To make the polenta, in a pot or large saucepan, combine the polenta, salt, butter, and 3 cups (710ml) water. Bring to a boil, stirring continuously. Once boiling, reduce the heat to low. Cook, stirring occasionally, for 20 to 30 minutes. If the polenta becomes too thick, add ¼ cup (60ml) water to loosen it up. When done, remove from the heat and cover to keep warm until ready to serve.

2   Meanwhile, prepare the shrimp. Peel the shrimp, placing the shells directly into a pot or large saucepan. Set the shrimp aside. Add 4 cups (1L) water to the shells and place over medium-high heat. Simmer for 30 minutes. Remove from the heat and let cool.

3   Heat a large, deep cast-iron pan over high heat. Add 1 tablespoon of the ghee and sauté the andouille sausage for 5 minutes or until golden brown. Do not stir. Remove the sausage from the pan and set aside.

4   Return the pan to the heat without cleaning. Add the shrimp, season with 2 tablespoons of the Cajun seasoning, and cook for 2½ minutes on each side. Do not stir. Remove the shrimp from the pan and cool with the sausage.

5   Reduce the heat to low; add the remaining 1 tablespoon ghee, onion, garlic, celery, bell pepper, and tomato, and sauté for 10 minutes until the vegetables are fully caramelized. Be sure to scrape up all of the browned bits at the bottom of the pan.

6 Sprinkle the flour and the remaining 2 tablespoons Cajun seasoning over the vegetables, stirring to coat them completely. Add about ½ cup (120ml) of the shrimp stock you've made to deglaze the pan, scraping up the browned bits from the bottom.

7 Add the remainder of the stock and bring to a boil. Once boiling, reduce the heat to a simmer and cook for 10 to 15 minutes. The mixture will thicken as it cooks and should have a sauce-like consistency.

8 Add the shrimp and sausage, and season with salt and pepper, plus more Cajun seasoning, if desired.

9 Before serving, warm up the polenta, and stir in the cheddar cheese and corn.

10 Serve the creole shrimp on top of the polenta and garnish with the oregano.

A dish like this is where the cast-iron pan really shines. Creole uses multiple proteins, all caramelized in the same pan, prior to deglazing and releasing all of those delicious flavors from the bottom of the pan. It's this layering of flavor that makes this dish so special.

MEATBALLS
WITH RICOTTA & TOAST

This dish is easy to serve family-style to a crowd, in a fun, everyone-help-yourself environment. It's also simple to make ahead—you prepare the delicious meatballs, sear them, freeze them, and take them along for the ride. When you arrive at your destination, all that's left to do is make a quick-and-easy sauce. The bright colors and flavors of the cherry tomatoes paired with the rich, meaty texture of meatballs and the creamy ricotta cheese makes a perfect spread for Italian bread.

FOR THE MEATBALLS:

3 tbsp olive oil, divided

½ yellow onion, finely diced

1lb (450g) ground beef

1 cup (90g) breadcrumbs

1 cup (100g) freshly grated Parmesan cheese

4 eggs

2 tbsp dried oregano

1 tbsp salt

½ tbsp pepper

FOR THE SAUCE:

½ head garlic, cut horizontally

2 cups (300g) cherry tomatoes

1 (12oz/340g) can tomato purée

Salt and pepper, to taste

TO SERVE:

1½ cups (375g) ricotta cheese

Basil leaves, to garnish

1 loaf good-quality French or Italian bread, sliced and toasted

1 Begin by preparing your heat source. You'll need a fire or stovetop burner set at medium-high heat. To make the meatballs, in a large skillet, heat 1 tablespoon of the olive oil. Add the onion and cook for 4 to 5 minutes or until translucent. Remove from the heat and cool.

2 In a large bowl, combine the ground beef, breadcrumbs, Parmesan cheese, eggs, oregano, salt, and pepper. Add the cooled onions. Using your hands, mix until well combined. Form the mixture into 16 to 18 medium-sized meatballs.

3 In a large cast-iron skillet over medium-high heat, heat the remaining 2 tablespoons olive oil. Add the meatballs and cook for about 10 minutes, searing on all sides until golden brown. (If making ahead, cool the meatballs completely, transfer to a freezer-safe bag, and freeze for later use.) Remove the meatballs and set them aside.

4 To make the sauce, place the halved garlic head in the skillet cut-side down. Add the cherry tomatoes around the garlic and cook for 5 to 10 minutes until the tomatoes blister.

5 Add ½ cup (120ml) water and the tomato purée, and season to taste with salt and pepper. Add the meatballs and simmer for 10 minutes or until thickened. Before serving, top with spoonfuls of the ricotta cheese and garnish with the basil leaves.

6 Serve with the toasted bread.

Many choose to roast their meatballs in the oven prior to putting them into their sauce. While I agree that this is very convenient, it does have a drawback. By searing your meatballs in the same skillet you make the sauce in, you gain all of that delicious savory flavor without dirtying an additional dish. Keep it in one pan if you can.

SERVES: 4 | PREP: 30–45 MINUTES | COOK: 1–1½ HOURS GF

STUFFED PEPPERS

This recipe reminds me of growing up because my mom made these peppers weekly. I also grew used to eating them regularly when I lived in the Middle East, as you become accustomed to eating stuffed vegetables often in that part of the world. These peppers are stuffed in the Middle Eastern fashion, with the rice left uncooked. Americans tend to think you have to cook the rice prior to stuffing the peppers. Not true. By using twice the amount of wet ingredients to rice in the mixture, the rice will steam-cook inside the peppers.

Olive oil

8 red bell peppers

1lb (450g) 70 percent lean ground beef

½ white or yellow onion, finely diced

1 (15oz/425g) can black beans, drained and rinsed

1 (15oz/425g) can corn

1 (10oz/283g) can red enchilada sauce

1 cup (190g) uncooked jasmine rice

Salt and pepper, to taste

Chopped fresh cilantro, to garnish

1 Begin by preparing your heat source. You'll need a fire, a grill, or an oven preheated to 350°F (180°C).

2 Coat a medium roasting pan with the olive oil. Set aside.

3 Cut off the tops of the bell peppers and set them aside. Hollow out the peppers, removing the membranes and seeds with a spoon, and set aside.

4 To a large bowl, add the ground beef, onion, black beans, corn, enchilada sauce, and jasmine rice.

5 Thoroughly fold the ingredients together, breaking up the beef into small pieces. The mixture should be very wet and paste-like.

6 Add a pinch of salt to the inside of each empty pepper, and stuff the peppers to the brim with the mixture.

7 Cap the peppers with the cut-off tops, arrange them in the prepared roasting pan, and cover. (Use aluminum foil if your pan doesn't have a lid.)

8 Roast the peppers over a fire, on a grill at medium heat, or in a preheated oven or Dutch oven for 1 to 1½ hours. Ensure that the lid or foil is well sealed so the peppers can steam. Don't rush the process with too much heat, as you can burn the peppers before the rice is fully cooked.

9 Once the moisture from the meat mixture is fully absorbed by the rice, the stuffed peppers are ready. Remove from the heat source, season with salt and pepper, garnish with cilantro, and let cool until it's ready to eat!

The uncooked rice soaks up all the delicious flavors during the cooking process and ultimately tastes much better. This style of cooking is known as "dolma."

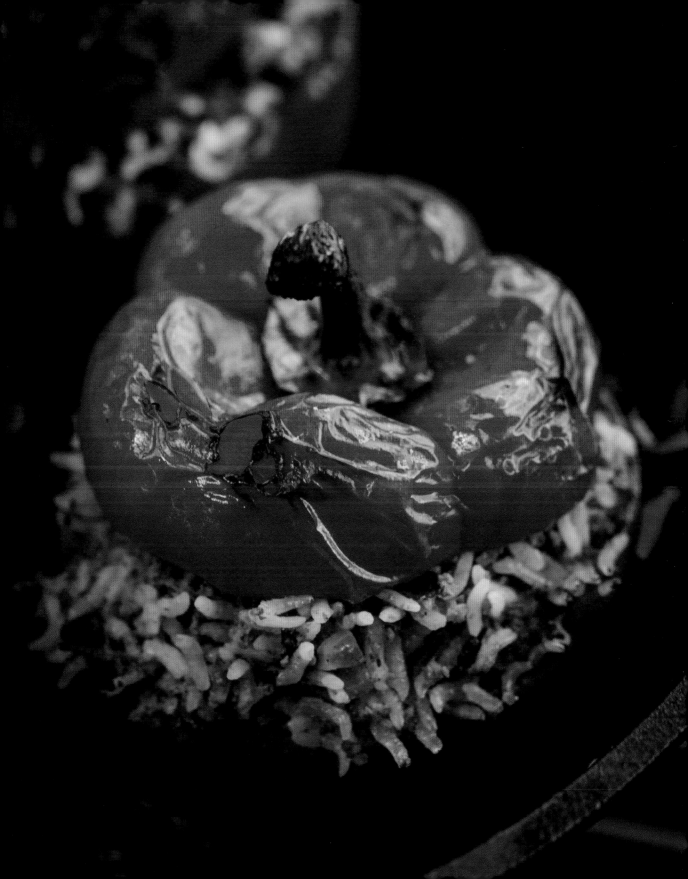

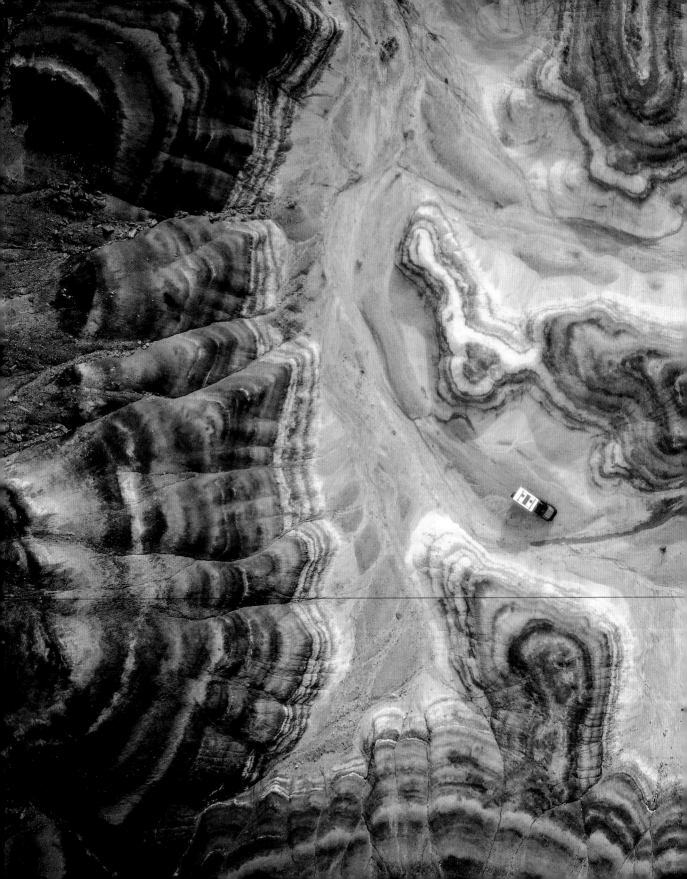

BE PREPARED

It's better to have it and not need it than to need it and not have it. This is generally the mentality I have when I go camping. Being prepared is something I began doing back in my Boy Scout days. I took my preparedness so seriously I eventually became an Eagle Scout, and now it's the focus of this chapter. Preparation is more of a lifestyle choice than you may realize, as you must make certain choices to always be prepared and to have things ready when you need them. It's also important to only bring items you absolutely need. This will save you time, space, and money. To achieve this, you've got to think about what you'll need in advance and create an action plan prior to heading out to your destination.

When it comes to cooking, being prepared often has more to do with your ingredients than your equipment. When your food is sufficiently prepped, you're able to spend more quality time with your friends and family and less time sweating over a hot fire. This kind of preparation can include everything from freezing stews in advance, to bringing premade soups with you, to precooking carnitas for the tacos you plan to make later that evening. Taking care of these items at home can help alleviate the stress of creating things from scratch on the spot. Not to mention, many recipes actually taste better the day after you make them. People often say leftover chili tastes better the following day, so why not plan ahead to experience this for yourself? This is also a great way to utilize your leftovers and make them taste even better—all you have to do is warm them up.

You can also prep by pickling or preserving ingredients. These types of ingredients are exactly the kind of items you want to bring with you on an excursion. They don't go bad, are shelf-stable at room temperature, won't take up any excess space in your refrigerator, and work as excellent little roadside treats. Premade pickled onions and jam preserves are convenient (and delicious) additions to meals you're making on the go.

In this chapter, you'll find recipes like Omelet in a Jar, which is an easy way to prepare your breakfast in one self-contained vessel, making it ready to whip up at any moment. By using this approach, all you have to do is quickly fire up a pan and simply pour out some of that omelet mixture. Within a few minutes, your friends and family are eating breakfast. Likewise, premaking the Chocolate Pan "Cakes" and keeping them refrigerated or frozen eliminates the need for a bowl or mixing or cleaning. You'll easily be able to pull out the dessert ingredients and make the recipe within minutes. After cooking dinner, no one likes to do too much work to make dessert.

Everyone in my family agrees that Mama's Chicken & Dumplings is better the next day, having had time to rest and chill in the refrigerator overnight. This concept also applies to being prepared, as you can bring that chicken and dumplings—fully cooked, chilled, and tasty as ever—ready to heat up and eat at your campsite in minutes. And remember, being prepared doesn't just apply to cooking outdoors or at your campsite. It's equally important at home or in a commercial kitchen. When you are prepared, your time in the kitchen or over the fire will be more enjoyable and less stressful.

Easy ways to be prepared:

- Have a specific menu in mind and only bring the ingredients and equipment necessary for those recipes.

- Make a list of your ingredients and equipment, and check it twice.

- Pack your ingredients in a way that considers preservation and shelf stability.

- Wrap herbs in newspaper or a moist paper towel to keep them fresh.

- Wrap tomatoes and other fragile ingredients in newspaper or paper towels to protect them from bruising.

- Refrigerate only the ingredients that absolutely have to remain cold.

- Use jars and Tupperware to store premade items, making them easy to bring on your travels.

- Consider as many dry, shelf-stable ingredients as possible.

- Store your ingredients in a way that's secure, and fill in any empty spaces with a dry towel to prevent your food from rolling and moving around, which could destroy it.

- Think about the space where you'll be cooking and prep your station accordingly.

- Always keep these basic staples on hand: salt, pepper, olive oil, and butter.

- Make dry food storage space a priority for items like rice, pasta, jarred and canned goods, sauces, and condiments. These items don't go bad easily and help make putting an amazing meal together more convenient. By designating a spot for these kinds of dry items, you can focus on acquiring meat and produce, with ample space for them to go in the refrigerator.

- If you plan to cook over a fire, bring a fire starter. Finding fuel to burn is generally easy—it's getting the fire started that's often the difficult part. Having a fire starter like tortilla chips, pitch wood, or just a bundle of dry sticks on hand is imperative to getting a quick-and-easy fire going. You can also use the paper you wrapped your vegetables in to start the fire, which helps eliminate waste.

- If you missed a step in being prepared, improvise and be willing to try new things.

OMELET IN A JAR

The omelet in a jar has to be the best thing that ever happened to camp breakfast. It's as simple as preparing everything for the omelet, including cooking your vegetables and meats. Place all your ingredients in a jar and store in the refrigerator. Or don't, and use them right away. It's just a fast and easy way to dish out incredible omelets effortlessly when out and about. I also believe the egg takes on more of the flavor from your sautéed ingredients, which just makes it taste better. You could also pour this mixture over some crispy potatoes to make a quick hash.

½ cup (65g) finely diced yellow onion

½ cup (75g) finely diced green bell pepper

12 eggs

1 cup (120g) grated cheddar cheese

½ cup (100g) diced tomato

2 tsp salt

1 tsp pepper

Sliced green onions, to garnish

1 Begin by preparing your heat source. You'll need a fire or a stovetop burner set at medium heat.

2 In a large, nonstick skillet, sauté the onion and bell pepper until translucent. Remove from the heat and let cool.

3 Into a large mason jar or other vessel with a tight-fitting lid, crack all the eggs. Add the cooled onion and bell pepper along with the cheese, tomato, salt, and pepper. Secure the lid tightly and then shake vigorously until the ingredients are thoroughly combined. The egg mixture can be used immediately or stored in a cool place (like a fridge or cooler) until it's time to serve up some omelets.

4 Place a large, nonstick skillet over the heat. Give the jar a shake to mix any ingredients that have settled, and then pour about one-quarter of the mixture into the pan. It should just cover the bottom of the pan. Cook for 1 minute, and then push the cooked eggs to the back of the pan, allowing the uncooked egg on top to roll forward and begin cooking. After 1 more minute, flip the omelet and repeat until the omelet is fully cooked.

5 Remove from the pan and repeat to make 3 more omelets. Garnish with green onions and serve.

If left in the refrigerator for multiple days, that's okay. The egg mixture will separate and look rather unappetizing. I can assure you, give it a good shake and the mixture will return to its original appearance and will taste no different. You do not have to use a glass jar. Use any leak-resistant vessel.

FIRE-ROASTED SALSA

Salsa is great to make in advance because it saves time and effort once you get to your destination, freeing you up to just enjoy what you made and spend time with those you're traveling with. The smoky flavors come from the roasted vegetables, and the taste only gets better the longer it's stored.

6–7 Roma tomatoes

2 jalapeños

½ white onion

3–4 green onions

5 limes

½ bunch fresh cilantro, rinsed and roughly chopped

Salt and pepper, to taste

1 Begin by preparing your heat source. You'll need a fire, a grill, or a stovetop burner set at medium-high heat.

2 Place the tomatoes, jalapeños, and white onion directly over the heat source. Roast the vegetables until they're lightly charred and the tomatoes have burst. They should reduce in size by one-third. This will take 10 to 15 minutes, but a quick 5-minute char works well too if time is tight. Finish by placing the green onions over the heat source for just a few minutes, as they will char up quickly.

3 Remove the fire-roasted vegetables from the heat and roughly chop the vegetables. De-stem the jalapeños and remove the seeds depending on how spicy you want the salsa. The more seeds you remove, the less spicy it will be. Once prepped, add the vegetables to a blender or food processor.

4 Use the pulse feature to chop up the vegetables until all the ingredients are mixed and incorporated.

5 Squeeze in the juice from the limes and add the cilantro.

6 Pulse the ingredients a few more times. Add salt and pepper to taste. It's important to let this salsa sit or be refrigerated, so try making it in advance, and remember to bring it with you wherever you're headed.

I often find when I make a recipe, it's sometimes less enjoyable if eaten right away. It's almost as if I need to walk away from it for a day or two and taste it later on to really appreciate it. This salsa is no different. Trust me, you'll enjoy it more if you let it sit for a bit.

JALAPEÑO POPPERS

These poppers are fun and easy to make because you can prep the kebabs before you leave the house. Cooking kebabs later at your campsite is super convenient when you bring them preassembled. Using kebab sticks will hold the wrapped poppers together without needing to use a toothpick for each popper, which can make the bacon shrink and expose the cheese, causing it to leak out during the cooking process.

8oz (227g) plain breakfast sausage

½ white onion, finely diced

14 jalapeños

2 cups (240g) grated cheddar cheese

1 (8oz/226g) package cream cheese

12 slices of bacon

Jam or honey, for dipping

1 Begin by preparing your heat source. You'll need a fire, a grill, or an oven preheated to 325°F (160°C).

2 In a large sauté pan, cook the sausage for about 15 minutes. Make sure it's well crumbled. Add the onion and cook until translucent, about 5 minutes. Drain any excess fat from the meat and set aside.

3 Slice the tops off the jalapeños and remove the seeds using the handle of a spoon.

4 In a large bowl, combine the cheddar cheese, cream cheese, and cooked sausage-and-onion mixture.

5 Place this mixture into a resealable bag and cut off the corner to create a piping bag. Squeeze the mixture into each pepper, filling them one by one.

6 Wrap the peppers with bacon. Use the fatty, wider end of the bacon to seal off the open end of the jalapeño. Using a finger, hold it there while you wrap the bacon all the way down the pepper.

7 Skewer through both ends of the bacon, and repeat for all the peppers, securing the bacon in place.

8 Roast the assembled bacon-wrapped peppers over your fire, on the grill, or in the oven on a sheet pan until the bacon has completely rendered.

9 Remove from the heat and let cool. Drizzle with the jam or honey or use the condiments for dipping.

You can use this method to prepare all different kinds of kebabs!

ROASTED BEET & GOAT CHEESE SALAD
WITH CANDIED NUTS

When you know what recipes you're planning to make before you go, you have an idea as to what your menu on the road is going to be. This recipe might seem like it's going to be complicated and require everything but the kitchen sink, but it's actually quite simple and easy to make. By carrying staple ingredients like honey, sugar, and nuts, you can be prepared to make a range of recipe mélanges. Because only the goat cheese and lettuce need to be refrigerated for this recipe, it goes to show how using staple ingredients frees up space in your cooler!

3 small red beets, stalks trimmed

1 tbsp olive oil

1 cup (125g) whole walnuts, shelled

1 tbsp honey

1 tbsp granulated sugar

1 tsp cayenne powder

1 tsp paprika

1 tsp curry powder

1 tsp salt

1 package mixed greens (arugula or spinach-based mix)

½ cup (4oz/120g) goat cheese

Balsamic vinaigrette, for dressing

1 Begin by preparing your heat source. You'll need a fire or an oven preheated to 400°F (200°C).

2 In a medium pan or skillet, coat the beets in the olive oil, cover, and roast for at least 45 minutes or until soft and easily pierced with a fork. Larger beets can take up to 2 hours.

3 Remove the beets from the heat source, let cool, and peel under cold water. Chop into bite-sized pieces and set aside.

4 To a medium bowl, add the walnuts, honey, sugar, cayenne, paprika, curry, and salt. Mix well.

5 Spread the candied nuts evenly onto a sheet pan and bake until golden brown and aromatic, 10 to 15 minutes. Remove from the heat source and let cool.

6 Plate the mixed greens and top with the roasted beets, candied nuts, and goat cheese. Drizzle with the balsamic vinaigrette.

Having a basic idea of what you want to make before you make it will help you at the grocery store and when storing foods. It also helps you to be more clearheaded, which will allow you to be a better cook overall.

WHITE FISH & PUTTANESCA

This is a great recipe to make in advance before you hit the road. You can also easily bring the jars of ingredients with you to make it on the go. Either way, you'll be prepared. Using jarred goods like the ones listed here makes a very convenient, hassle-free, long-lasting meal that won't take up any extra space in your fridge. Little to no cleanup is necessary after you've made this dish, which is another part of the beauty of being prepared.

2lb (1kg) white fish (any white fish works)

12–15 cherry tomatoes

2 tbsp olive oil, divided

½ white onion, diced

4 garlic cloves, minced

1 (12oz/340g) jar kalamata olives, pitted and roughly chopped

1 (12oz/340g) jar green olives, pitted and roughly chopped

1 (12oz/340g) jar roasted red peppers, roughly chopped

1 (8oz/228g) jar capers

1 (4oz/113g) can tomato paste

Salt and pepper, to taste

Fresh dill, to garnish

1 Begin by preparing your heat source. You'll need a fire or a stovetop burner set at medium-high heat.

2 Clean your fish by removing any bones, and portion the flesh into four 8oz (227g) fillets.

3 In a large skillet that's been preheated over your heat source, blacken the cherry tomatoes with a touch of olive oil for 3 to 4 minutes.

4 Add the diced onion and garlic, and sauté until translucent.

5 Add the olives, peppers, and capers.

6 Stir in the tomato paste.

7 Add 2 cups (480ml) water and season with salt and pepper. Mix until all ingredients are thoroughly combined.

8 Let the mixture simmer uncovered for 15 minutes or until the sauce begins to thicken. Taste and add more salt and pepper if needed.

9 Rub the fish with a little olive oil, and evenly coat with salt and pepper.

10 Place the fish fillets into the sauce so they're about two-thirds of the way covered with the sauce. Cover with a lid or aluminum foil to poach over medium-low heat for at least 5 minutes or until the fish is fully cooked. Thicker pieces of fish might take up to 10 minutes. The fish will easily flake with a fork when it's done.

11 Remove from the heat source and garnish with the dill.

You can cook the sauce in advance and bring it with you or simply open the jars on site, chop up the ingredients, and make the sauce. All you'll have to do to complete the recipe is drop the fish in.

MAMA'S CHICKEN & DUMPLINGS

This is my great-grandmother's recipe, and it's always served at our family gatherings. The beautiful thing about having parts of this recipe previously prepared is that there's no cooking needed on site to finish it. All you have to do is quickly reheat it. This is also one of the most delicious and easiest meals you can make as you roam freely. Bringing your ingredients already prepped will save you a lot of time.

3 cups (360g) all-purpose flour

1 tsp salt

6 tbsp vegetable shortening

2 large eggs

1 whole roasted chicken

2qt (2L) chicken broth (preferably homemade; see recipe on page 27)

½ cup (120g) heavy whipping cream or full-fat milk

Salt and pepper, to taste

Fresh thyme, to garnish

1   Begin by preparing your heat source. You'll need a fire or a stovetop burner set at medium-high heat.

2   To make the dumplings, in a large bowl, combine the flour, salt, and shortening until the mixture is crumbly.

3   Add the eggs and ⅔ cup (156ml) water to the flour mixture, and combine thoroughly.

4   Turn out onto a floured work surface and knead until smooth. Let rest for at least 20 minutes.

5   Roll out the dough until relatively thin, about ¼ inch (6mm). Dust with flour and cut into little rectangles, about 1 x 2 inches (2.5 x 5cm).

6   Shred the chicken into large pieces with your fingers. (The bones can be used to enhance your broth if using store-bought.)

7   In a large pot, combine the chicken broth and shredded chicken.

8   Bring to a boil over medium-high heat and add the dumplings. Reduce the heat and simmer for 30 to 40 minutes. The dumplings will be floating and firm when they're ready.

9   Thoroughly stir in the cream or milk to complete the chicken and dumplings.

10 Season with salt and pepper, and garnish with the thyme.

Bring any frozen soup or stew with you. It can work like an ice pack to keep your fridge or cooler colder even longer.

CHOCOLATE PAN "CAKES"

One way to be prepared is by using a flour that already has leavening agents mixed in. This makes it quick and easy to create fun and interesting new dishes. From breads to cakes and crumbles, this kind of flour can be very useful, saving you time and effort. One bonus is that pancakes are very easy to freeze and store well. These "cakes" can be made in advance and stored for later use if you need a quick dessert idea. They travel very well and can be a surprising treat during your next outing. To freeze in advance, simply let each cake completely cool to room temperature. Cut 2 to 3 pieces of parchment paper into 6-inch (2.5cm) squares. In a zip-top bag, place a cake, then a piece of parchment, then another cake, and continue the process until the bag is full. Freeze and enjoy at a later date.

½ cup (50g) cocoa powder

⅓ cup (40g) self-rising flour, such as Bisquick

1 large egg

2 tbsp butter, melted, plus more for the pan

⅓ cup (66g) granulated sugar

1 tsp salt

⅓ cup (80ml) water or milk

TO SERVE:

Fresh berries

Whipped cream

Chocolate flakes

Powdered sugar

1 Begin by preparing your heat source. You'll need a fire or a stovetop burner set at medium heat.

2 In a large bowl, combine the cocoa powder, self-rising flour, egg, melted butter, granulated sugar, salt, and water or milk. Mix until a smooth batter forms; it should resemble brownie batter.

3 In a large cast-iron skillet, melt enough butter to coat the bottom of the pan. It should be lightly sizzling.

4 Just like you're making pancakes, drop a few spoonfuls of batter into the skillet, taking care not to overcrowd the pan. Cook for 3 to 5 minutes. When bubbles begin to form and pop on the surface, flip the cakes. Cook for 1 to 1½ minutes on the opposite side and remove from the pan. Repeat this process until all the batter has been made into cakes.

5 Serve topped with berries and whipped cream and sprinkled with chocolate flakes and powdered sugar.

When making these, it's slightly more challenging than just a sturdy ol' pancake. These are gooier and more delicate. I always err on the side of a very well-greased pan. If the heat is too high, you'll likely add a burned flavor to the chocolate. So keep it at medium and be patient.

EQUIPMENT

The equipment you have at your disposal does not necessarily dictate what you can cook. It's more about how you use the equipment you do have. I can make cakes without an oven, soups without a blender, and pizza without a pizza oven. The real challenge is learning to be flexible with the equipment you do have, and applying ingenuity to get the job done in the easiest possible way. As a professional chef who has worked in small spaces for over a decade, I've perfected the art of minimizing dirty dishes and keeping a clean work station, all while creating elaborate dishes within the confines of my limited kitchen space and equipment. By overcoming these limitations and learning a great deal across my adventures cooking outdoors and over a fire, I've found the pieces of equipment that are the most versatile for cooking both indoors and outdoors.

The average cook seems to believe that a kitchen gadget can be their savior. The way I see it, these gadgets are often only one more thing to clean. If you can find a way to use just a cutting board and knife, your prep and clean time will be cut in half. By finding ways to use one bowl instead of two, or a fork instead of a whisk, you can make your time spent in the kitchen more enjoyable and less stressful.

A chef's knife can work as an extension of your hand. It's the most important piece of equipment we have in our kitchen toolbox. I try not to stray far from this concept, often using nothing more than a great knife kit, a couple of basic pots and pans, and a heat source. All those other gadgets might seem like they're saving you time and making your life easier, but often they only create more fuss.

If I could only choose one piece of equipment, it would have to be a sharp, quality knife. A good portion of the frustrations I see people encounter in the kitchen involves their dull, neglected knife. You can't dice a ripe tomato with a dull knife. Many people don't realize the way ingredients are cut or sliced affects how your palate interacts with the final dish. A sharp, quality knife paired with refined knife skills allows you to seamlessly prep your food and take the overall caliber of the dish to the next level.

If you have limited kitchen space or storage, consider using a cook set. Cook sets include a stock pot, sauce pot, and skillet. Many of them can stack and collapse into themselves, too. A cook set contains everything you need within the smallest possible footprint. These are available in both cast iron and stainless steel.

Smoker

Cast-Iron Skillet

Folding Peeler & Parer

Meat Thermometer

Griddle

Folding Chef's Knife

Portable Pizza Oven

Folding Camp Utensil

Cowboy Tripod

The equipment used in this chapter includes the basics I cannot cook without. If you're seeking to equip your culinary adventure properly, then follow these guidelines and leave all the extra gadgets behind.

Only bring the equipment you need. Plan accordingly when traveling and cooking. I typically have a general understanding of the recipes I plan on preparing, whether at home or on the go. The recipes I plan to prepare ultimately determine what equipment will be needed.

Equipment to always have with you:

TOOLS

- 6- to 8-inch chef's knife
- 6- to 8-inch boning knife
- peeler
- zester or microplane
- grater
- spatula
- long pair of tongs
- ladle
- cutting board
- dry rags and/or leather gloves
- mixing bowl
- measuring cups and spoons

POTS AND PANS

- large cast-iron skillet with lid
- cast-iron flat top
- stock soup pot
- Dutch oven
- cookie sheet

The importance of cast iron:

- Cast iron is commonly used when cooking outdoors, and there's a reason why. The primary purpose for using cast iron over a camp fire is to ensure heat retention. Cooking outdoors presents a lot of variables that can pose a challenge for even the most experienced chefs. Obstacles like shifting wind, an unpredictable heat source, fluctuating temperatures, and falling rain could all quickly dampen your cooking experience. But if you're using cast iron, the thick metal can hold on to heat even if the temperature of your fire fluctuates.

- Cast iron can also reach higher temperatures than most of its counterparts. This allows you to sear, caramelize, blacken, and develop levels of flavor and texture that no other pan can easily produce. In addition, cast iron holds up well to these high temperatures (especially those of a camp fire), preventing warping or damage. It also lasts a lifetime.

- Another added benefit of using cast iron is that you don't have to add soap to clean it. You simply scrape it clean with steel wool and water, dry it immediately, and coat it with oil.

ROSEMARY SMASHED POTATO BREAKFAST HASH

A breakfast hash is an excellent way to feed a large number of people. The crunchy potatoes and big chunks of breakfast sausage are filling and the perfect way to get the day going. When I'm feeding large numbers of people, I lean into equipment like the flat-top griddle. This large, flat piece of iron holds a steady temperature and rarely has hot spots. If you're considering adding the perfect cast-iron edition to your kitchen arsenal and you don't yet have a flat-top griddle, I highly recommend you get one. The large cooking surface allows you to prepare vast quantities of food quickly, from breakfast hash to fried rice to the perfect smash burger. There's something special about cooking over a flat top for large quantities of people. It has that teppanyaki feel, with the steam rolling in front of your face while you manipulate the food to perfection right before your eyes.

8–10 small Yukon Gold potatoes

1lb (450g) ground pork breakfast sausage

½ white onion, diced

1 green bell pepper, diced

2 tbsp butter

2 tsp salt

1 tsp black pepper

3 sprigs rosemary, leaves only, minced

1 Begin by preparing your heat source. You'll need a fire or a stovetop burner set at high heat.

2 In a large pot of boiling water, cook the unpeeled potatoes for 20 minutes or until cooked through. A fork should easily pass through the entire potato when fully cooked. Drain and set aside.

3 Heat a flat-top griddle or a large cast-iron skillet over medium heat. Add the sausage and cook, stirring frequently, for 10 minutes or until the sausage is crumbly and golden brown.

4 Add the onion and bell pepper. Continue cooking for 5 minutes.

5 Push all the ingredients to the back of the griddle, creating a clear, hot zone to fry the potatoes. Add the butter to the cleared area and place the boiled potatoes onto the griddle.

6 Using a rigid metal spatula, carefully smash down the potatoes to flatten them somewhat. (Remember, you're not making mashed potatoes.) Let the potatoes cook without flipping for 7 minutes. Do not stir; simply let them caramelize. Slide your spatula underneath to ensure that they are not sticking to the pan. This will also help the caramelization. When the potatoes are crunchy on the bottom, it's time to flip them.

7 Flip the potatoes and distribute the sausage mixture across the skillet. Cook for 5 minutes more, and finish with the salt, pepper, and rosemary.

If you don't have a flat griddle or grill pan, you can use an electric griddle or a large cast-iron skillet. Be sure to use gold or red potatoes, as they hold up better than Russet potatoes with this cooking technique.

PANZANELLA

A good, sharp knife is the single most important tool for the chef because this tool becomes an extension of the hand. This is one of those recipes where having a good knife is key, allowing you to effortlessly cut through each ingredient, resulting in beautiful, appealing edges for your panzanella salad. The importance of good knife skills will show when it comes to the final appearance of this salad, which can be a showstopper. And always remember, a sharp knife is a safe knife!

1 whole loaf artisan bread

½ cup (120ml) olive oil, divided

1 tsp salt

2 cups mozzarella (1lb/450g), cut into cubes

1 large cucumber, peeled and diced

½ red onion, thinly sliced

20–25 cherry tomatoes, cut in half

Salt and pepper, to taste

A few sprigs fresh basil, to garnish

Balsamic reduction, to drizzle

1 Begin by preparing your heat source. You'll need a fire, a grill, or a stovetop burner set at medium-high heat.

2 Cut your bread loaf into ¾-inch (2cm) cubed chunks, about the size of extra-large croutons.

3 Coat a large skillet with ¼ cup olive oil, add the bread cubes, and cover generously with salt. Toast until golden brown on all sides, about 10 minutes, and remove them from your heat source.

4 To a large bowl, add the bread cubes, mozzarella, cucumber, onion, and tomatoes. Toss all the ingredients with more olive oil and mix thoroughly until every ingredient is coated.

5 Finish with salt and pepper to taste. Garnish with the basil and drizzle with the balsamic reduction.

This can also make a composed salad if you choose to not toss or mix it and instead plate the ingredients neatly and symmetrically in rows.

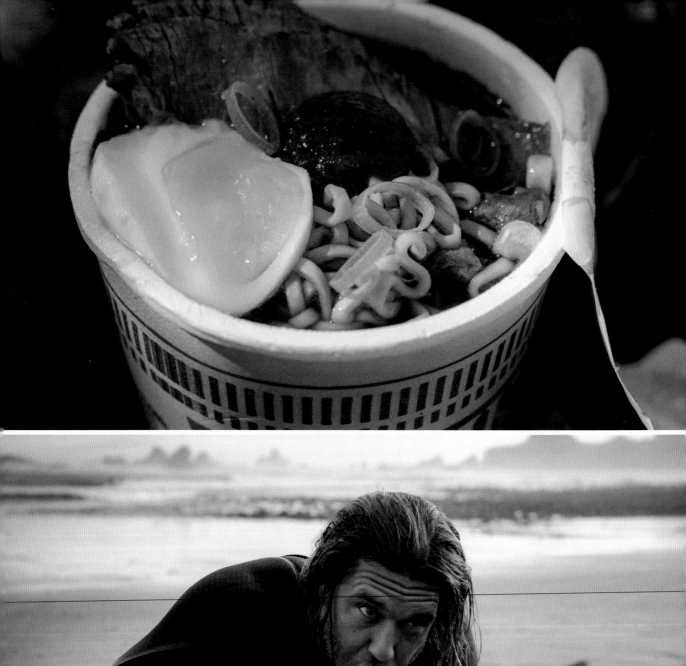

BRAISED BEEF CAMP RAMEN

There's no shame in doctoring up a cup of instant noodles. Bring some braised beef with you to camp, and you'll have a decadent, rich, and inspired cup of ramen in just the amount of time it takes to warm up the meat. I often travel with bone broth that I make at home, which makes it much easier to quickly enhance the flavors of this dish. If you don't want to go through this trouble, simply bring bouillon cubes or reduced broth in a jar.

1lb (450g) boneless beef short ribs

3 cups (710ml) beef bone broth

2 eggs

2 (2.25oz/64g) cups instant ramen noodle soup (with the packet of flavor removed and discarded from each)

1 green onion, sliced, to garnish

Sriracha (optional), to garnish

1 Begin by preparing your heat source. You'll need a fire or a stovetop burner set at medium-high heat.

2 Place a large, lidded pot over medium-high heat. When hot, add the beef and sear for about 5 minutes on each side until golden brown.

3 Add the broth and bring to a simmer. Reduce the heat to low, cover, and simmer until the beef is tender and falling apart. This will take 3 hours for a whole cut of meat.

4 When ready to serve, add 2 eggs with the shell still on to the pot to be soft boiled. Cook for 5 minutes. Remove the eggs from the pot, peel them carefully, and set aside.

5 Add the boiling broth to a cup of noodles. Replace the lid and let sit for 3 minutes or according to the package instructions. You can also use packaged ramen noodles instead.

6 When the noodles are fully cooked, add the sliced or shredded beef. Slice the eggs vertically and place two egg halves in each cup. Garnish with green onion and serve with a drizzle of sriracha if desired.

Allowing the whole cut of beef to simmer for 3 hours is the best way to develop rich, robust flavor. However, if you're short on time, you can cube the beef and decrease the cook time to about 1½ hours. I recommend cooking it whole, though—it's just better.

MY PERFECT PIZZA

Pizza is one of those dishes that can either be amazing or really bad. This is often the case with recipes that use very few ingredients because those ingredients need to be quality or the whole pizza will be off. Great pizza has three important components: dough, sauce, and cheese. For this recipe, you should source fresh mozzarella, make Roma tomato sauce, and be sure to create your own pizza dough. In my opinion, the dough is the most important part, and the longer you let it rise, the better it will turn out. If you're the proud owner of a pizza oven, this is a great time to use it. A pizza stone is an excellent alternative if you'll be making pizza on a grill or in an oven.

FOR THE DOUGH:

1 tbsp active dry yeast

1¼ cups warm water

1 tbsp olive oil

1 tsp sugar

2 tsp salt

3½ cups (420g) all-purpose flour (½ cup [60g] extra for dusting)

FOR THE SAUCE:

5 Roma tomatoes, quartered

2 tsp salt

FOR THE TOPPINGS:

1lb (450g) whole-milk mozzarella

1 cup (100g) shaved or grated Parmesan cheese, (¼ cup reserved)

12 slices prosciutto

3 handfuls arugula

1 In a large bowl, combine the yeast, warm water, oil, and sugar. Mix until the yeast has bloomed and smells fragrant, about 5 minutes.

2 Add the salt, then mix in the flour one cup at a time. You can use a stand mixer or hand mixer for this, but I typically just do it by hand, using a fork as my dough hook.

3 Once the dough is pulling away from the walls of the bowl, stop mixing. Lightly coat the dough with the reserved flour and cover with a moist towel. Let rise for the next 3 to 4 hours at minimum. The longer you let it rise, the better. I let mine rise overnight in the refrigerator.

4 Once the dough has risen, remove from the bowl and punch it down in the center. Re-form the dough into a large ball to be portioned.

5 Cut the dough into 2 to 3 fist-sized balls, doing your best to shape them into equal spheres.

6 Cover the dough balls one last time for their final rise. Once they've risen for another 20 minutes or so, they're ready to be turned into pizza!

7 While the dough balls rise, prepare your heat source. You'll need a pizza stone if using a grill or standard oven. You can place the stone directly on your grill or oven rack, preheated to 500°F (260°C). If using a pizza oven, set to 600° to 700°F (315° to 370°C).

8 To make the sauce, add the tomatoes and salt to a medium sauce pot and simmer on medium-low. Smash the tomatoes with a fork periodically until the sauce reaches a consistent smoothness, like a thin paste.

9   To make the pizza, sprinkle a little flour onto a cutting board and place a dough ball in the center. Work the dough ball from front to back with only your fingertips to push any excess air out.

10   Using lightly floured hands, pick up one side of the dough and let gravity start to stretch it. Continue a rotating motion, holding the dough at the top, until your pizza dough reaches your desired thickness.

11   Place the dough directly onto your pizza stone or prep surface and top with an even layer of sauce, then a light layer of the cheeses.

12   If using a pizza oven, bake the pizza for 10 minutes, hot and fast. If using a grill or standard oven, it will take closer to 20 minutes. The crust should look and feel crunchy.

13   Remove the pizza. Top with the sliced prosciutto, a handful of the arugula, and add more Parmesan cheese if desired.

> My best advice is to practice working with dough often, as it can take some getting used to in the beginning. The best way to learn is to play around with making fresh dough yourself. Maybe even try watching some pizza-making tutorials! And be sure to keep in mind that the hardest part of making a good pizza is making good dough, so once you've mastered that, you'll be all set.

TRISKET

I love this smoked tri-tip because it provides a brisket-like texture to what is otherwise a temperamental and often tough meat to cook. Owning a pellet smoker or smoker can be a rewarding experience, but don't feel like it's the only way to prepare this meat. If you don't own a smoker, that's okay because you can slow-cook this in an oven too. You can have all the outdoor cooking devices in the world, but that won't guarantee you'll be able to create a succulent, mouthwatering meat.

1 whole untrimmed
    tri-tip (1½–2½lb/
    680–1135g)
½ cup (115g) salt
¼ cup (35g) pepper
Barbecue sauce
    (optional)

1 Begin by preparing your heat source. You'll need to get your smoker set to 215°F (100°C) or an oven preheated to 225°F (110°C).

2 The fat cap (the side of the meat with more fat) should remain fairly thick, as this is what will keep the tri-tip moist as it cooks, but you can trim off any excessive chunks of fat from the tri-tip.

3 Coat the tri-tip with a generous amount of salt and pepper.

4 Smoke the tri-tip on the top rack for 10 hours. If using an oven, skip to step 7.

5 After 10 hours in the smoker, you've created the smoky outside crust known as the pellicle. Now you need to finish cooking the meat without drying it out. Wrap it tightly with butcher paper if you have it. You can also use plastic wrap followed by foil.

6 Place the meat back into the smoker until the thickest part of the meat has an internal temperature of 200°F (90°C). This can take 2 to 3 hours more.

7 If using the oven, cut your tri-tip into 2-inch (5cm) squares. Place the squares in a casserole dish or cast-iron pan with walls, and slather them in barbecue sauce if desired. Cover with aluminum foil and slow-cook in the oven for 3 to 4 hours or until they're fall-apart tender. Toss them on the grill to get a nice char on the outsides to finish, another 5 to 10 minutes.

8 Once the trisket is ready, remove it from whichever heat source you used, and let it rest for at least 20 minutes before slicing into it. When slicing into just about any cut of meat, you want to do it against the grain. Run your knife perpendicular to the grain and slice into equal cuts.

Making mouthwatering meat dishes requires some basic understanding of protein cookery, specifically the kind of protein you're choosing to cook and how. The equipment you choose to cook the meat will determine the method by which you apply the heat.

CHICKEN-FRIED STEAK & GRAVY

Chicken-fried steak might be my favorite thing ever. It is the very first dish I remember learning how to cook. It's tradition for my dad and me to order and rate it at every restaurant we go to that offers it. This heavy, roll-me-away-in-a-wheelbarrow meal is a devilish treat that I fix for myself most birthdays. Its nostalgic presence in my life meant that it needed to be in this book for that reason alone. Serve alongside mashed potatoes and corn on the cob to complete the experience.

FOR THE STEAK:

1½ cups (180g) all-purpose flour

¼ cup (40g) cornmeal (optional)

½ cup (65g) cornstarch

1 tbsp salt, plus extra

1 tbsp pepper, plus extra

4 eggs

2 cups (470ml) cooking oil (peanut oil preferred)

4 cube steaks, each about 8oz (225g)

FOR THE GRAVY:

8 tbsp butter

½ yellow onion, finely diced

1½ tbsp all-purpose flour

2 tsp salt

1½ cups (350ml) whole milk or half-and-half, at room temperature

A few sprigs thyme, tied into a bundle using kitchen twine

1 Begin by preparing your heat source. You'll need a fire or a stovetop burner set at medium-high heat.

2 In a shallow dish, mix the flour with the cornmeal (if using), cornstarch, 1 tablespoon salt, and 1 tablespoon pepper. In a second shallow dish, whisk the eggs with a splash of water.

3 In a large cast-iron skillet, heat the oil over medium-high heat until it reaches 350°F (180°C). If you don't have a thermometer, test the temperature by adding a pinch of flour to the oil. If it sizzles and floats right away, you're ready to go; if it's smoking it's too hot.

4 Season each steak generously on both sides with salt and pepper. Dredge the steaks one at a time, using one hand to dip each steak first in the flour, then into the beaten egg, then back into the flour, pressing it in with your hand.

5 Once fully breaded, the steaks are ready to fry. Carefully add them to the hot oil and fry for 3 to 4 minutes until golden brown. Flip the steaks and fry for 2 to 3 minutes more. Remove from the oil and transfer to a plate lined with paper towels. Cover to keep warm until ready to serve.

6 To make the gravy, drain off the cooking oil, leaving just a tablespoon in the pan. Reduce the pan to medium heat and melt the butter. Add the onion and cook until completely translucent, about 10 minutes.

7   Sprinkle with the flour and salt and mix thoroughly, forming a roux. Stir in the room-temperature milk and thyme, and simmer for 5 minutes or until thickened. Remove the sprigs of thyme.

8   Serve the gravy over top of the chicken-fried steak, accompanied by mashed potatoes and corn on the cob if desired. Garnish with the thyme leaves.

While this isn't the most small-space-friendly of dishes, it is an exercise in how to use your tools and make sure you have the basic equipment required to cook any meal. If you can haul this recipe into the great outdoors, like the chuck wagons before us, you'll be able to make anything.

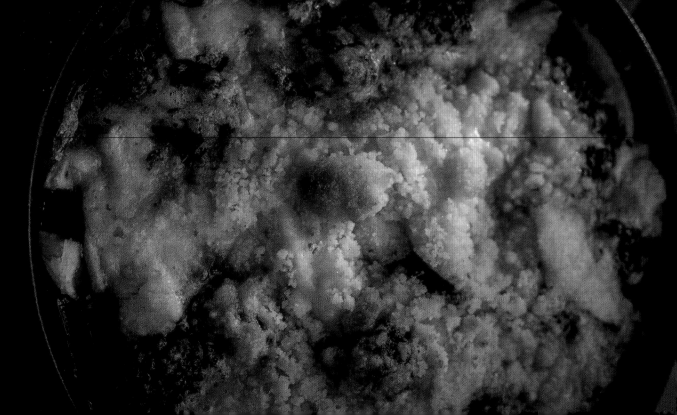

BERRY APPLE COBBLER

Summertime desserts like this one are sure to be a hit. Road-tripping through the Pacific Northwest in late summer can bring this dish to life. To be able to forage all the fresh fruits needed to create this dessert is such a treat. For me, it's not only the incredible summertime flavors but also the mouthfeel that makes this dessert special. The crunch of the baked streusel topping and the fresh fruity foundation to the cobbler is the perfect summertime treat.

FOR THE BASE:

1½ cups (225g) blackberries

1½ cups (285g) blueberries

1½ cups (190g) raspberries

1 green apple, peeled and diced

Zest and juice of 1 lemon

2 tsp pure vanilla extract

¼ cup (55g) brown sugar

¼ cup (50g) granulated sugar

Pinch of salt

FOR THE TOPPING:

½ cup (55g) all-purpose flour

½ cup (100g) granulated sugar

Pinch of salt

Pinch of ground cinnamon

½ stick melted unsalted butter (plus extra)

1 Begin by preparing your heat source. You'll need a fire or an oven preheated to 300°F (150°C).

2 Butter a Dutch oven or a large, oven-safe baking dish. Set aside.

3 In a large bowl, gently mix together the blackberries, blueberries, raspberries, and green apple.

4 Add the lemon zest, lemon juice, and pure vanilla extract. Coat with the sugars. Add a pinch of salt. Mix thoroughly until all the ingredients are evenly coated.

5 Transfer the mixture to the Dutch oven if using a fire (or the baking dish if using an oven). Set aside.

6 To a separate large bowl, add the flour, sugar, salt, and cinnamon. Mix thoroughly to combine.

7 Slowly add the melted butter to the bowl, and use a fork to mix it in with the other ingredients. When large crumbles begin to form, stop adding the butter.

8 Heavily coat the top of the berry casserole mixture with the crumble mixture, using a wooden spoon to spread evenly. Cover with a lid.

9 If using a fire, place the Dutch oven overtop of it and carefully add hot coals atop the Dutch oven lid. Keep it at a consistent medium-heat level for 20 to 30 minutes.

10 If using the oven, place on the low rack and bake until the berries have burst and the top layer is golden brown. This should take 25 to 35 minutes.

11 Remove from the heat source, let cool, and enjoy!

> If you're not in the Pacific Northwest on a road trip, that's okay. You can make this dish with the fruit available at your local grocery store, farmers market, or fruit stand.

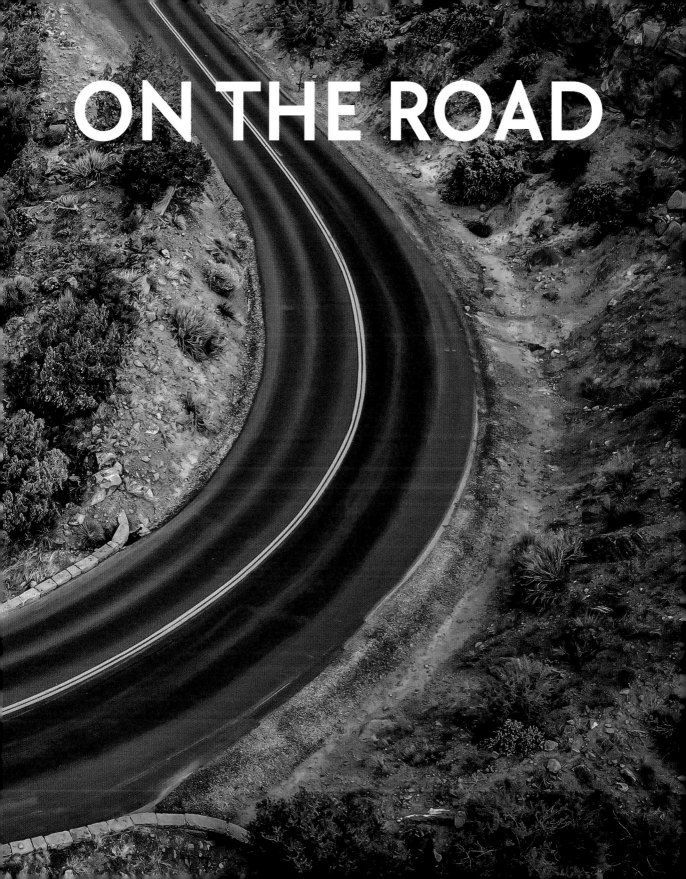

ON THE ROAD

A nomadic lifestyle has long been a part of the human experience. We go where the resources are. When those resources are depleted, we move on to the next spot. It's deeply embedded in our DNA to want to see new things, to smell something different in the air, to find an untouched environment to settle in, or to face new challenges. It wasn't until our recent modern civilizations took hold that we became complacent and happy staying put behind a white picket fence.

Our ancestors were the best road trippers the world has ever seen. Depending on the availability of food, water, and the ever-changing climate, whole communities of indigenous peoples had to be fully mobile. They did not have the option to stay in one place. They had to move. I believe we still have these tendencies to keep moving, but we often feel trapped in the cities where we reside. We are meant to be boundless and explorative, and when you spend too much time in the comforts of your home, you deprive yourself of the chance to grow from new challenges. It's my goal to encourage you to tap into the nomadic nature of our ancestors and get a taste for what a mobile life has to offer. So please, be as nomadic as your life will allow.

In recent years, especially in the aftermath of the COVID-19 pandemic, life on the road has become incredibly popular. Some people have sold everything and hit the road to explore our beautiful country. With fewer ties and obligations, you can focus your attention on the open road and the next place you want to see, all while sourcing the goods and ingredients you need from the local communities you visit along the way.

You don't need a built-out Sprinter van and every piece of gear known to man to have a meaningful experience on the road. All you need, really, is the willingness to get outside and see new things. Just don't forget to bring the best ingredients with you.

When you sit down to enjoy one of these recipes with an epic landscape stretching out before you, I am sure you will feel an immense sense of satisfaction and accomplishment. There's something special about taking the chance to leave everything behind and pursue life out on the open road. And the nice thing is, you can always choose a place you like to stay put once you're ready to settle down. Living a more unattached and mobile lifestyle gives you the chance to feel what life is like without all the bullshit, so I urge you to try it out.

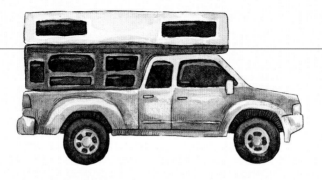

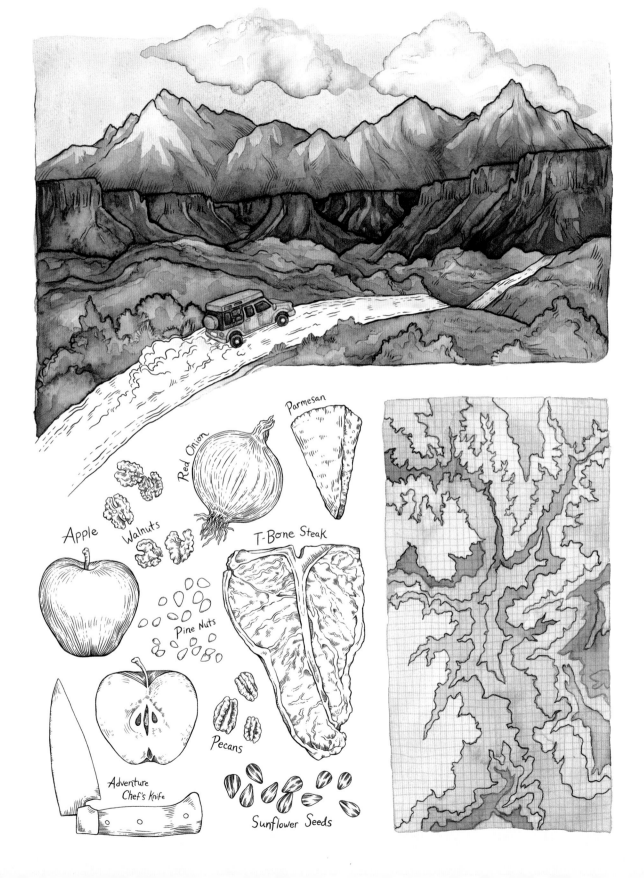

Parmesan

Red Onion

Walnuts

Apple

Pine Nuts

T-Bone Steak

Pecans

Adventure
Chef's Knife

Sunflower Seeds

My life on the road began when I was in my early twenties as a blossoming yacht chef. The jobs I had on boats were often unpredictable. They could range in length from two weeks, to two months, to two years. These jobs made it so I had no real need for a home in the traditional sense. I lived on a boat full time, but this came with access to the marina's parking lot, pool, spa, gym, showers, and bathrooms. These amenities covered everything I needed to live in my vehicle whenever I was off the boat. And believe me, I definitely needed time off the boat in order to stay sane. Time to surf, camp, and be by myself.

This life on the road has been more than twenty years in the making. At twenty-four years old, I purchased a used Econoline (a windowless work van) for $6,000 in cash. From that day forward, my life changed forever. I drove from San Diego to Seattle, up to Vancouver, British Columbia, and eventually made it all the way to Alaska, where I ultimately left the van.

For those who feel lost or are looking for something more, you might not find it sitting at home. Adventure allows you to find yourself. If you adventure solo, like I have for the past twenty-five years, you'll end up doing some serious introspection. For many years of my adult life, I didn't know what having roots was like until I bought my first mattress in my mid-thirties. All I knew was life on the water or on the road. That's how nomadic my life has been.

"Home is where the heart is" is a famous saying for a reason. In my experience, the road really shows you where your heart is. It exposes what you love and hate, and helps you realize how much stuff you really don't need. I find it often takes a minimum of two weeks living on the road before you truly embrace the nature of uncertainty that comes along with it. It's usually around this point in your journey that you give in to the idea that you don't necessarily need to have a plan or destination in mind. You can take it mile by mile, simply deciding if you want to go right or left when a fork appears in the road. This feeling of lawlessness, absolute freedom, and raw decision-making is sure to make you feel alive and forget why you would even need to have a traditional home in the first place.

JUNIPER JUICE

The berries of the juniper tree are commonly overlooked. We drive and hike past them all the time, and many don't realize these are the same berries used to ferment gin. I wanted to see if we could make a quick, fermented drink using the same principles as kombucha. The white powdery substance that naturally coats fruits and berries is actually yeast. When this yeast is combined with sugar, it creates carbon dioxide. When given enough time, the natural yeast from the juniper berries and the honey will create an effervescent delight. Familiarize yourself with what a juniper berry looks like so the next time you're on a road trip, you might be compelled to grab a handful of berries and put them in a jar with a scoop of honey. Then wait for your little science experiment to produce a natural, refreshing beverage.

1 cup fresh juniper berries

½ Honeycrisp apple, thinly sliced

2 tbsp honey

1 Place the juniper berries, apple, honey, and 2½ cups (½L) distilled water (not city tap water) into a sealable 16-ounce (470ml) mason jar or any other similarly sized airtight vessel.

2 Give it a good shake and let it rest at room temperature in a shaded place for up to 7 days.

3 The drink can be consumed within hours of making it, but more flavor will develop over time, and eventually a nice bubbliness will be achieved through the fermentation process.

This recipe is best when fully fermented after 3 days have passed. Leaving the jar sealed and unopened allows the natural yeast on the berries and honey to react and create gases, adding a nice effervescent pop to the beverage. If you don't have the time to wait, you can still use this recipe to create delicious, flavor-infused water in minutes.

JALAPEÑO PEACH MARMALADE

When I'm on the road, I absolutely love to pull over to enjoy a good view and a snack. It's so satisfying to have the ingredients for this recipe readily available, and the beautiful thing is they don't really go bad. In fact, they're even better at room temperature. Make this spicy peach jam before you head out on your next road trip, and take it with you to elevate your roadside charcuterie board to the next level.

10 jalapeños, sliced into rounds ¼ inch (6mm) thick

½ white onion, finely diced

1 (1lb/450g) can sliced peaches in syrup (or 4–5 overripe fresh peaches, sliced)

¼ cup (60ml) apple cider vinegar

1 cup (200g) granulated sugar

Salt and pepper, to taste

1 Begin by preparing your heat source. You'll need a fire or a stovetop burner set at high heat.

2 Bring a saucepan of water to a boil and add the sliced jalapeños. Boil for 10 minutes. (This will remove most of the intense heat from the peppers.) Drain.

3 In a large saucepan over medium-high heat, sauté the onion for 3 to 5 minutes or until translucent.

4 Add the jalapeños, peaches, apple cider vinegar, sugar, salt, and pepper. Cook over medium heat for about 30 minutes or until the mixture has reduced by a third and the liquid easily coats the back of a spoon.

5 Remove from the heat and let cool completely. At room temperature, it should be a thick, spreadable consistency.

6 Consume right away with manchego cheese and crackers or jar it up and save for a later date. Store in a jar in the fridge for 3 to 4 weeks. If properly canned, it will stay good for up to a year.

Some like it hot, some like it mild. You can adjust the heat index of your marmalade by boiling the jalapeños for half the time. Or not at all. The important thing is that you use the whole pepper, including the seeds.

HOMEMADE BEEF JERKY

To me, nothing says "road trip eats" like beef jerky. Unfortunately, the majority of beef jerky sold in the United States is overpriced and not particularly tasty. When you make your own, you'll save money and enjoy the flavor and texture much more. Jerky can be made in a smoker, on a grill, in the oven, or in a dehydrator. Whatever method you choose, the process is the same: cook the meat on low until it's lost most of its moisture content. So fire up the pellet smoker, oven, or grill and get to making some jerky.

2–3lb (1–1.4kg) beef sirloin

1 cup (240ml) Worcestershire sauce

Salt and pepper, to taste

1 Begin by preparing your heat source. You'll need to get your smoker or grill preheated to 180° to 200°F (80° to 90°C) or an oven to 225°F (110°C).

2 Cut the meat into slices 6 to 8 inches (15 to 20cm) long and ½ inch (1.25cm) thick.

3 In a large bowl, layer the beef strips, seasoning each layer with Worcestershire sauce, salt, and pepper.

4 Once the meat has been thoroughly seasoned, let it marinate for 10 minutes.

5 Cook the meat for approximately 3 hours or until the jerky looks dark in color, is firm, and pulls apart easily. Remove from the heat source and allow it to cool completely.

6 Transfer to plastic zip-top bags, pressing out as much air as possible, or seal using a vacuum sealer. Vacuum-sealed jerky can be frozen for up to 8 months.

By purchasing a large cut of sirloin and slicing it yourself, you'll increase your savings of price per pound with smoked meats like jerky.

BILTONG

I learned how to make biltong after years of feeding South African crew members on various boats. The South African people have a strong influence in the marine industry, and it became essential to learn their cuisine. One of the most requested dishes was a simple snack known as biltong. This African delight is nothing more than air-dried cured beef. Once you've had one piece, you won't be able to stop. It's virtually nuclear bomb proof and only requires air and time to be cured correctly. This recipe is unique because although raw meat is left out at room temperature for weeks, it will still be perfectly safe to eat. The curative properties of vinegar and salt are enough to prevent bacteria growth and even deter flies. It's the perfect roadside snack. Simply bring a big chunk of biltong and slice off a piece when you need a quick bite of something tasty.

½ cup (40g) whole coriander seeds

1 cup (230g) coarse salt

¾ cup (165g) brown sugar

1/3 cup (45g) black pepper

3lb (1.4kg) bottom round steak (any steak works)

1/3 cup (80ml) Worcestershire sauce

½ cup (120ml) red wine vinegar

MATERIALS:

6 paper clips

1 In a dry skillet over medium heat, toast the whole coriander seeds for about 5 minutes until lightly browned and fragrant. Once toasted, remove from the heat. Do not let them burn.

2 Place the toasted seeds into a mortar and pestle or a sturdy plastic zip-top bag. If using the plastic bag method, use the back of a saucepan and a flat surface to grind the seeds. (You can also use a food processor or blender.) Pulverize the seeds until the texture reaches a small-to-medium grind. Do not overprocess into a powder.

3 Add the salt, sugar, and pepper to the ground coriander and mix well. Transfer the spice mixture to a rimmed baking sheet or shallow pan and spread it out in a thick layer.

4 Place one steak at a time into the spice mixture. Lightly press, flip, and press again. Repeat for each steak.

5 With all the steaks lying flat in the pan or baking sheet, pour the Worcestershire sauce and red wine vinegar around the steaks. Do not pour directly over the steaks to avoid washing off the spices. Flip each steak in the liquid to fully coat prior to marinating.

6 Place the baking sheet or pan into the refrigerator to marinate. Marinate thinner steaks for a minimum of 6 hours. Steaks that are thicker than 1½ inches (4cm) should marinate for up to 12 hours. Flip steaks halfway through marinating.

7 Meanwhile, find a place to use as a drying rack to hang the steaks. You can use a window, a closet rod, a clothes rack, or even make a "biltong box" for future use. All that matters is that the space where the meat is hung is at room temperature and well ventilated. Reshape the paper clips into S-hooks to prepare them for hanging on your rack.

8 Remove a steak from the marinade, gently shaking off any excess liquid. Thread one of the paper clip hooks through the meat, placing it at the tip but not too close to the edge. Hang the steak on the rack or hanging space you're using and place a few paper towels or a rag below to collect drippings. Repeat the process for all steaks.

9 Leave the meat hanging to dry for up to 2 weeks. Thinner cuts might be ready in 10 days or less.

10 Biltong is ready when the exterior is nearly black in color and the interior of the thickest part of the meat is ruby red. For wetter biltong, remove from the rack earlier. For drier biltong, let it dry for longer. Thinly slice and enjoy.

> If no refrigeration is available to you during the marinating process when camping or you only have limited refrigerator space, that's okay. The meat can marinate at room temperature because the salt and acidity will prevent bacteria growth.

APPLE CHICKEN SALAD

When I'm on the road, I like to eat things that are relatively healthy, but when I stop at gas stations, they often have the worst food. I've seen questionable chicken salad sandwiches in the cold foods section way too many times, so I decided to make a much better version of this dish to enjoy on the go. Recipes like this are great because all you need for a full meal is some bread, crackers, or lettuce, and you're off to the races for an awesome lunch.

1 whole roasted
   chicken,
   deboned

1 red apple, diced

2 ribs celery, diced

½ red onion, diced

1½ cups (185g)
   chopped pecans

1 bunch tarragon,
   finely chopped,
   plus more to
   garnish

2 tbsp Dijon
   mustard

3 tbsp mayonnaise

Salt and pepper, to
   taste

1   Begin by preparing your heat source. You'll need a fire or an oven preheated to 400°F (200°C).

2   Remove the meat from the chicken with your hands, shred, and place in a large bowl.

3   Add the apple, celery, and red onion to the bowl.

4   Briefly toast the pecans in the oven on a baking sheet or in a skillet over the fire. Remove from the heat source, let them cool, and add to the bowl.

5   Add the tarragon, mustard, mayonnaise, and salt and pepper to taste.

6   Mix all the ingredients thoroughly to create the chicken salad. Once combined, place in the fridge to let cool for at least 1 hour.

7   Serve with fresh bread, as a sandwich, on top of greens, or just eat as is.

This recipe keeps very well in the cooler or fridge and will last for a while. So be sure to hang on to any leftovers for a convenient snack.

PESTO & GOAT CHEESE FOCACCIA

When I was younger, I went on a road trip with my dad and we brought a bag full of cold pizza slices. Ever since then, I've loved eating pizza or bread when I'm on the road. This focaccia is the perfect driving food, as it's easy to eat with one hand, creates very little mess, and always satisfies my cravings. Make this in advance and slice it up for a convenient, ready-to-eat, refrigeration-free snack whenever you need it. It can also work as a bit of comfort food when you're feeling tired from being on the road all day and you want something with a cozier vibe.

FOR THE DOUGH:
3 tsp instant yeast
2 cups (475ml) warm water
2 tsp salt
4 cups (480g) bread flour, plus more for dusting
Olive oil

FOR THE TOPPINGS:
½ cup (120ml) olive oil
½ cup (125g) prepared pesto
½ red onion, thinly sliced
½ cup (120g) crumbled goat cheese
¼ cup (35g) pine nuts
½ cup (100g) grated Parmesan cheese
Balsamic glaze, to garnish
Basil leaves, to garnish

1 To make the dough, in a large bowl, combine the yeast and water. Using a fork, mix in the salt and add the flour a little bit at a time.

2 When the dough has come together and is mixed thoroughly, cover with a clean, damp dish towel and leave the dough out in a warm place for 1 to 2 hours or until it has risen and doubled in size. It should feel soft and wet to the touch.

3 Turn the dough out onto a lightly floured surface and knead until it's smooth and elastic. Generously coat a large cast-iron skillet or baking sheet with the olive oil and transfer the dough into the vessel. Cover with a damp dish towel, and let rise again at room temperature for 2 to 3 hours.

4 When ready to bake, prepare your heat source. You'll need a fire, a grill, or an oven preheated to 400°F (200°C).

5 Drizzle a little olive oil onto the dough, and with your fingertips, spread the dough evenly to fill the pan.

6 Top the dough with hefty spoonfuls of pesto, and press them in with the spoon. Sprinkle the sliced onion, goat cheese, pine nuts, and Parmesan cheese evenly over the surface of the dough.

7 After adding the toppings, let the focaccia rise for 10 to 15 minutes before baking. Bake for 25 to 35 minutes or until the crust is golden brown.

8 Drizzle with balsamic glaze and garnish with basil before serving.

Toss sliced focaccia into a hot skillet for a few minutes and have a warm meal with a crunchier crust than the first time!

SMOKED FISH SANDWICH

Smoking is an excellent way to preserve the fresh fish you've caught on your adventures, and smoked fish salad travels well as long as you keep it cool. When I was sailing across the Pacific Ocean, we caught a massive 400-pound marlin and I had no place to put all the meat we harvested from it. We pulled up to the nearest little island, set anchor, and I spent the next 24 hours smoking all the meat. Long story short, we were eating smoked fish sandwiches like this one regularly.

**FOR THE
SMOKED FISH:**

At least 2lb (1kg)
white fish fillets

½ tbsp salt

**FOR THE
SALAD:**

1½lb (680g)
smoked white
fish (prepared as
directed or
store-bought)

1 rib celery, finely
diced

¼ cup (32g) finely
diced red onion

A few sprigs dill,
chopped

Zest and juice of
2 lemons

¼ cup (60ml) olive
oil

2 tbsp mayonnaise

**FOR THE
SANDWICHES:**

Sliced sourdough
bread

Sliced tomato

Sliced red onion

Red leaf lettuce

1 To make the smoked fish, preheat a smoker to 200°F (90°C). Salt the fish generously, and smoke for about 2 hours. Cook times will vary depending on the type of fish and thickness of the fillets, so begin checking the fish after 1½ hours. The fish is done when it reaches an internal temperature of 160°F (70°C) or is very firm to the touch.

2 To make the salad, in a bowl, combine the smoked fish, celery, onion, dill, lemon zest and juice, olive oil, and mayonnaise. Mix thoroughly. I like to leave some large chunks of fish in mine. Refrigerate until ready to use.

3 To assemble the sandwiches, spread a large portion of the fish salad on the bread and top with sliced tomato, onion, and lettuce. Serve with a side of potato chips.

Smoking fish is a fantastic preservation technique to continue eating fresh fish weeks down the road. Keep that smoked fish refrigerated or frozen in large chunks and use as the base for dips, soups, and sandwiches like this.

SOUTHWESTERN CHICKEN PASTA

This recipe was inspired by my travels through Texas, where my family has roots. Texans have a way of adding that southwestern flair to just about everything they eat. That means: chiles, lime, and tequila. These flavors shine in this spicy, smoky pasta salad, which relies on shelf-stable items that can be stored at room temperature while on the road, saving precious space in your coolers and refrigerators.

3 slices bacon

5 garlic cloves

½ cup (120ml) tequila

1 (4oz/113g) can green chiles

1 (15oz/425g) can black beans, drained and rinsed

1 (15oz/425g) can whole kernel corn, drained and rinsed

1 (3oz/85g) jar oil-packed sun-dried tomatoes, drained

2 cups (480ml) whipping cream

Salt and pepper, to taste

1lb (450g) bowtie pasta (farfalle)

1 cup (16g) fresh cilantro, leaves only, chopped

¼ cup (60ml) lime juice

1 whole roasted chicken, deboned, skin removed, shredded

1   Begin by preparing your heat source. You'll need a fire or a stovetop burner set at medium heat. In a large, deep-set skillet or saucepan, cook the bacon for 5 minutes or until it is golden brown and the fat has rendered. Remove the bacon from the pan when it is fully cooked and dice into small pieces. Set aside.

2   Add the garlic to the pan and cook for 15 seconds. Add the tequila to deglaze the pan, scraping any browned bits from the bottom.

3   Add the green chiles, black beans, corn, sun-dried tomatoes, and whipping cream. Season with salt and pepper, reduce the heat to low, and simmer for 20 minutes.

4   In a large pot of boiling salted water, cook the pasta according to the package instructions until cooked but still firm to the bite (al dente); drain.

5   Add the warm pasta to the sauce and stir in the chopped cilantro and lime juice. Add the shredded chicken and bacon. Give the pasta a good stir, folding gently to incorporate everything.

> If you do not have a rotisserie or roasted chicken available to you, chicken breasts, legs, or thighs work just as well. Either roast them yourself, grill them, or give them a quick poach in water or broth to cook through before adding to the pasta.

OVER A FIRE

Cooking food over a fire is directly linked to our history as a species. The day we began to cook over a fire was the beginning of modern civilization, in my opinion. Yet as our kitchens have become fancier and our refrigerators bigger, the technique and skill set behind cooking over an open flame has declined. In many industrialized cultures, the art form of gathering supplies, getting the fire going, and maintaining it for the duration of the cooking time has been all but lost through the conveniences of modern kitchens with their stoves that can be ignited with the flick of a switch or the turn of a burner knob.

Using an open flame is fine when you're using pots and pans, but when you place ingredients directly over a flame, you'll often coat the ingredient with black soot. This result is unappealing and unappetizing. That's why I recommended using heat from the coals alone when attempting to char various ingredients without a cooking vessel.

Your fire size will depend on the type of meal you're trying to cook. For example, if I'm making pancakes in the morning, I just need a hot cast-iron skillet for 20 to 30 minutes, as opposed to cooking a chili, which requires hours of steady heat. If I need a heat source for less than an hour, I stick to tinder and kindling and avoid logs altogether. They're just not necessary. By the time that log has fully burned, you'll have moved on from breakfast to lunch. Only create the amount of fire you need. If I know I'm cooking all day or need a particularly large amount of coals, I'll use logs. In this process, I'll often have two fires: one for burning down logs and creating coals, and another for doing the cooking. By shoveling hot coals into your secondary pit, you'll have a better cooking experience because you'll avoid flare-ups and uneven temperatures.

Before we discuss the process of building a fire, it's important to know the rules of fire safety. Be aware of fire restrictions and necessary fire permits in the area. You'll need a minimum twenty-foot-diameter space free of any flammable debris. In the center of that cleared space, gather rocks, cinder blocks, bricks, or anything you can get your hands on that's fire-resistant. Use these items to create a pit, which will contain your fire and coals. Always have something on hand you can use as an extinguisher, such as a bucket of water or a shovel to bury the fire with dirt to smother it. You can never be too sure your fire has been extinguished. Double-check and then triple-check it. You'll know your fire is completely extinguished when you can touch and hold your hand to the coals. All it takes is one stray ember to start a forest fire and it's easier than you might think. Never leave your fire unattended. The image on pages 126–127 is a perfect example of what not to do. While it looks cool, every little spark could lead to a potential forest fire.

Types of Campfire:

teepee

log Cabin

Star

lean-to

Council

1. Tinder

2. Kindling

3. Logs

TYPES OF TINDER: TWIGS PINECONE DRY PINE NEEDLES BARK

KINDLING: TWIGS NO THICKER THAN PINKY

SMALLER LOGS → BIGGER FIRE

Here are three guidelines to follow if you're new to or struggling with how best to cook over an open fire.

1. **Gather.** Much like gathering your ingredients for a recipe, you need to gather the ingredients to make a proper fire. You'll need these three things:

   a. **Tinder.** This can include dry pine needles, leaves, paper towels, newspaper, cardboard, pine resin, sticks, twigs, pine cones, cattails, and tortilla chips (my personal favorite). These items can help provide the biggest flame from the smallest source. A good friend of mine once said, "Small wood makes big fire."

   b. **Kindling.** This is a medium-sized piece of wood, though it should be larger than your tinder. Kindling should be small enough to easily catch fire on all sides and large enough to continue burning until a bed of coals is created to ignite larger logs.

   c. **Logs.** These are the pieces of wood that are large enough to provide hours of heat, but take the longest to catch fire. So don't think you can start your fire with just a log, or even three. These are for extended use only after you have developed a hot bed of coals to ignite them.

   However much wood you think you're going to need, bring or gather three times that amount. Cooking over a fire requires quite a bit of fuel, and it's easy to underestimate how much you'll need. It's better to have it and not need it than to need it and not have it.

2. **Ignite.** How you ignite your fire determines the speed and efficiency at which it begins to burn. Contrary to popular opinion, I like to get my fire going before building any sort of structure with wood. I'll use one medium-sized log in the center of my fire pit to provide elevation for all my little sticks and tinder. It's the elevation of your fire starter material that allows a high flow of oxygen. This abundance of oxygen helps the fire breathe and gain momentum, furthering its ability to ignite the next piece of wood. A common mistake when attempting to get a fire going is smothering the fire with too much wood. This excessive amount of material prevents adequate airflow, which disables the fire's ability to burn.

   Begin with only a small amount of tinder paired with a fire starter. Once lit, allow the tinder to fully ignite before adding any kindling. When you observe a steady flame, add one piece of kindling at a time, being careful not to smother the fire. This slow and steady addition of kindling guarantees the hot bed of coals needed to maintain a steady burn.

3. **Cook.** As if cooking in your kitchen isn't difficult enough, doing it over an open flame can seem downright impossible. But don't be discouraged, it's not as difficult as you may think. You don't need to go far to find yourself a suitable place to build a campfire. You can build one in your local park (rules permitting), your backyard fire pit, and of course, your next campsite. Cooking over a fire is really about temperature management. It is a constant dance between the food and the fire. Modern cooking allows us to simply turn a dial and reach a specific temperature. Turn that same dial, and the heat can be extinguished. Unfortunately, this modern convenience is not available when cooking over a fire. We have to raise and lower the temperature by raising and lowering either the food or the flame. This means you must either add fuel to your fire, or lower your food closer to the coals to achieve the desired result.

CHARRED SHISHITO PEPPERS

This is the kind of recipe that's so fast and easy, you'll likely be surprised by how satisfying it is. Simply bring a few ingredients with you, make a hot fire, and in minutes you'll be eating. The art of charring over the fire takes practice but it's very rewarding. This fire and this moment need your undivided attention; to walk away could be the difference between eating a delicious side dish or feeding the local wildlife.

1lb (450g) shishito peppers

Sesame seeds (optional), to garnish

FOR DIPPING:

1 tbsp grated ginger

1 tbsp grated garlic

½ cup (120ml) ponzu sauce

Flaky salt

1 Begin by preparing your heat source. You'll need a fire or a grill preheated to at least 500°F (260°C).

2 To make the dipping sauce, in a small bowl, combine the ginger, garlic, and ponzu sauce. Set aside.

3 Place the whole peppers on the grill. Using tongs, turn the peppers to grill on all sides until lightly charred black. Don't walk away from the grill! The peppers will char in 1 to 2 minutes per side.

4 Remove the peppers from the heat source and immediately sprinkle with flaky salt and garnish with sesame seeds (if using). Transfer to a serving dish and dress with ponzu. Serve warm.

This technique is all about having a hot grilling surface and keeping your attention on the peppers so they don't burn.

PROSCIUTTO-WRAPPED ASPARAGUS
WITH GOAT CHEESE

This fast and easy recipe hits all the major senses and makes a perfect little snack or appetizer. The salty, chewy crunch of the grilled prosciutto coupled with the tangy creaminess of the goat cheese, the sweetness of the balsamic glaze, and some smoky elements from the fire will leave your taste buds wanting more.

10 slices prosciutto

½ cup (120g) goat cheese

1 bunch asparagus, woody ends trimmed

1 tbsp balsamic glaze (optional)

1 Begin by preparing your heat source. You'll need a fire or a grill set at medium-high heat.

2 Lay out one slice of prosciutto on a worksurface. (Don't worry if it tears; the cheese will hold it together.)

3 At one end of the prosciutto, place a dollop of goat cheese.

4 Place 1 spear of asparagus on the goat cheese. (For thinner asparagus, use 2 or 3 spears.)

5 Roll the prosciutto around the goat cheese and asparagus so the prosciutto forms a casing around the cheese. Repeat these steps until all the prosciutto has been used.

6 Place on the grill over medium-high heat. Grill for 3 to 5 minutes or until the prosciutto is crisp, the cheese is melted, and the tips of the asparagus are lightly browned.

7 Drizzle with balsamic glaze for an additional layer of flavor if desired. Serve warm.

If you want your asparagus to be less crunchy, you can precook your spears for a bit before you assemble them with the prosciutto and cheese.

ROADSIDE ELOTE

Street food vendors around the world have embraced the fast and efficient method of cooking over fire because it provides the highest yield of flavor in the shortest period of time. Elote, a classic Mexican street food of grilled corn, perfectly balances the complex smokiness imparted by cooking over fire along with the sweetness of fresh corn. Cool and creamy cotija and mayo round out the dish.

10 ears of corn

8oz (227g) cotija cheese

¼ cup (25g) equal parts cumin and paprika

1 bunch cilantro, chopped

½ cup (115g) mayonnaise

Hot sauce, to taste

½ cup (120g) sour cream (optional), to garnish

Lime wedges, to serve

1 Begin by preparing your heat source. You'll need a fire or a grill set at medium-high heat.

2 To prepare the corn, remove the husk and corn silk. (I like to leave the stem attached for a handle.)

3 Bring a large pot of salted water to a boil. Quickly submerge the corn in the boiling water, 3 to 4 minutes.

4 Place the corn on the grill and cook for 10 minutes, turning the corn to achieve a char on all sides.

5 On a plate, crumble the cotija cheese, and add the spice mix and cilantro. Mix well to combine.

6 Coat each ear generously with mayonnaise and roll in the cheese mixture.

7 Top with the hot sauce, garnish with the sour cream (if using), add a squeeze of lime juice, and enjoy!

Ears of corn are another great example of durable foods that last a long time at room temperature and will easily make it to any campsite unscathed.

FIRE-ROASTED STEAK FRITES

I love cooking a steak on a rotisserie over an open fire. It allows the steak to cook low and slow, with just the right kiss of the flame to achieve the caramelization you're looking for without dirtying a pan. (Of course, you can also grill your steak or sear it in a cast-iron pan.) Pair your fire-roasted steak with campfire frites (fries) for a classic combination.

FOR THE STEAK:

1 tomahawk steak (bone-in rib eye), about 2½lb (1kg)

Coarse salt and pepper

8 tbsp butter

1 bunch sage

FOR THE FRITES:

3 Russet potatoes, peeled and cut lengthwise into ¼ inch (6mm) thick sticks

1–2qt (1–2L) cooking oil, for frying

Salt and pepper, to taste

3 garlic cloves, minced

2 tbsp chopped parsley

FOR THE STEAK:

1 Begin by preparing your heat source. You'll need a fire or a grill with a good base of coals to provide heat for up to 1 hour.

2 Thoroughly coat the rib eye with a coarse salt-and-pepper rub (more salt than pepper). Cook on a rotisserie or grill until the steak reaches an internal temperature of 125°F (50°C) for medium rare. Finish it with high heat to get the crispy bits and good caramelization.

3 Meanwhile, in a small saucepan, melt the butter, skimming off the white milkfat. Add the sage and let it simmer until ready to serve.

4 To serve, slice the meat off the rib and then cut it against the grain into ¼-inch (6mm) slices. Drizzle with the warm sage butter and serve with the frites

FOR THE FRITES:

1 Place the potatoes in a large pot of cold water. Bring to a boil and cook for 3 minutes. The edges should begin to look more translucent than the center. (They will not be fully cooked.) Drain. Let cool and dry for 10 minutes.

2 In a Dutch oven, heat the cooking oil to 350°F (180°C). Test for temperature by dropping in a piece of potato; the oil is hot enough if it floats and sizzles right away.

3 Slowly and carefully add the potatoes to the hot oil. Fry for 5 to 10 minutes or until golden brown. Using a slotted spoon or kitchen spider, transfer the frites to a bowl lined with paper towels.

4 Season with the salt, pepper, garlic, and parsley. Toss the bowl to coat the frites with seasoning.

Anyone can cook a great steak; it's making those perfect fries that's always the hard part. Rarely are we served truly fresh fries—potatoes and nothing else. By blanching the potato in water first we can ensure that the potato is completely cooked through on the inside, and crunchy on the outside, which also keeps them from sitting too long in the oil.

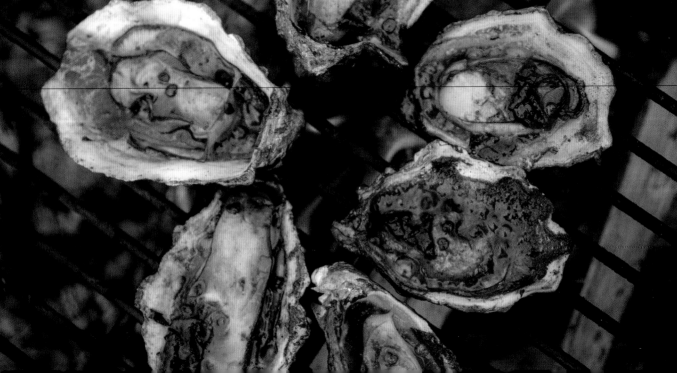

GRILLED OYSTERS
WITH CHIPOTLE HONEY BUTTER

This recipe was inspired by a good friend who is a third-generation oyster farmer. In Lilliwaup, Washington, deep in the Puget Sound, you'll find the Hama Hama Oyster Company, where the world-famous Blue Pool oyster was developed. It was here that I was introduced to the grilled oyster with various compound butter flavors. My favorite is their chipotle honey, but there's an endless variety of compound butter flavors that you can add to your oysters. A quick and easy chef trick is to make the compound butter in advance. Whether it be for this recipe, for the top of a steak, to finish your sauces, or to use in countless other ways, compound butter can be an excellent addition. Chefs prepare compound butter days, if not weeks, in advance, as it freezes very well. In the case of the adventurer, it travels incredibly well and makes a massive impact on the flavors of your next meal.

8 tbsp salted butter, at room temperature

1 (7oz/200g) can chipotle peppers in adobo (use just 2–3 tbsp of the sauce, or 2 of the peppers, minced)

2 tbsp honey

½ tsp black pepper

15–20 small to medium grilling oysters (whole, unshucked)

1 Begin by preparing your heat source. You'll need a fire with a large grilling surface or a grill set at medium heat.

2 In a medium bowl, combine the butter, chipotle peppers, honey, and black pepper. Mix thoroughly and set aside.

3 Place the oysters on the grill with the flat side facing down and curvy side facing up.

4 Cook over medium heat for 10 to 15 minutes, depending on the size of your oysters. You'll begin to see steam and the shells will open. You may need to assist in opening and removing the top shell using tongs and heavy-duty oven/grilling mitts. Certain oysters can be slow to open when steaming. (Another option is to simply place the oysters on their half shell directly on the grill. In this case, you would shuck them first.)

5 Place a dollop of the chipotle honey butter on top of each oyster.

6 Let oysters simmer in the butter for 2 to 3 minutes and no longer than 5 minutes. Serve warm.

When cooking over a fire, to determine cooking temperature, simply use the palm of your hand hovering over the fire. If you can hold it for 5 seconds, that's high heat. If you can hold it for 8 seconds, that's medium heat. If you can hold it for 10 to 12 seconds, that's low heat.

CARNITAS TACOS
WITH CRISPY QUESO TORTILLAS

Tacos are a nearly perfect camping food: they're fast, low key, inexpensive, and always a crowd-pleaser. You can find the ingredients at just about any grocer, and they all travel quite well. My favorite tacos are these ones that feature carnitas, as you can prepare the meat at home and bring it with you. This way, when you're hungry and ready to eat after a day spent outdoors, your food is basically already made. All you have to do is heat up a skillet and get to making those delicious cheesy tortillas. Warm up some meat, and you're ready to eat.

FOR THE CARNITAS:

2lb (1kg) boneless pork shoulder, cut into several large pieces

3 tbsp kosher salt

FOR THE TACOS:

1 white onion, finely diced

1 bunch cilantro, finely chopped

4 cups (400g) grated Monterey Jack cheese

16 small corn tortillas

2–3 green onions

5 limes, cut into wedges

Hot sauce (optional), to serve

1 Begin by preparing your heat source. You'll need a fire or an oven preheated to 300°F (150°C).

2 Salt the pork generously on all sides and place in a large Dutch oven. Cover with a lid and place over the fire or in the oven. Cook for 1½ hours or until the meat is tender and falling apart. Set aside to cool. When cool enough to handle, shred the meat. (Carnitas can be made ahead and kept refrigerated or frozen until ready to use. Thaw and reheat in a pan over medium heat until heated through.)

3 When ready to eat, prepare the toppings. In a small bowl, mix the white onion and cilantro.

4 Heat a large, well-seasoned cast-iron skillet or griddle over the fire or a stovetop burner set at medium heat. Place a small handful of cheese on the skillet, about the size of a tortilla. Let it cook for 2 to 3 minutes or until you're able to slide a spatula under it. Place a tortilla on top of each cheese pile and flip.

5 Meanwhile, add the whole green onions to the skillet to give them some char. Remove after 2 to 3 minutes and finely chop.

6 Assemble the tacos by piling the cheesy tortillas with shredded carnitas, onion, and cilantro. Add the chopped green onion, a squeeze of lime, and hot sauce.

> This recipe calls for less cheese than the incredible street tacos you can find in LA. That said, feel free to add a tall pile of cheese to make each tortilla. I love it when there is burnt cheese on the outside but still soft cheese on the inside.

WHOLE HEN ROAST

The perfect whole-roasted chicken has been kissed by a flame, resulting in a crisp golden skin, fall-apart tender thigh meat, and juicy breast meat. Spatchcocking, or removing the backbone, allows the bird to cook evenly on the grill. After that, it's all about temperature management and undivided attention. Very few ingredients are necessary—just patience and the perfect over-the-fire technique.

1 whole chicken, about 3lb (1.4kg)

2–3 tbsp olive oil or butter, plus more melted butter for basting

Salt and pepper, to taste

Lemon slices, to garnish

1 To prepare the chicken, remove it from the packaging and discard any giblets and the neck bone if present. Pat the chicken dry, place on a plate or baking sheet, and refrigerate uncovered for several hours. (This allows the skin to dry completely, which will help it crisp.)

2 To spatchcock the chicken, place it on a cutting board breast side down. Using kitchen shears, cut out the backbone. Starting from the tail end, cut up along one side of the backbone and then repeat on the other side. Flip the chicken over (breast side up) and press firmly on the breastbone to flatten the chicken.

3 Prepare your heat source. You'll need a fire or a grill with one side set at medium heat, about 350°F (180°C), and the other side cool.

4 Rub the chicken with olive oil or butter, and season liberally with salt and pepper to taste.

5 Place the bird on the cool zone of your lidded grill, skin side up. The bird should stay on the cool side the entire time it cooks and never be directly over the heat. Turn the chicken in place occasionally to get it evenly cooked on all sides.

Close the grill lid and cook for 1½ to 2 hours, basting the skin every 20 minutes with the melted butter. Maintain the temperature at 350°F (180°C). The chicken is done when the skin is golden brown and a gentle tug on a drumstick is enough to pull it out. An instant-read thermometer inserted into the thickest part of the thigh should read 155°F (68°C). It will continue to cook once removed from the heat source and should rise about another 10°F (5°C).

This is a low and slow process; there's no rush here. The longer you take, the better it will taste. The objective is to fully render the fat before the skin starts to burn, which is accomplished by temperature management. The bird should be positioned just barely close enough to be kissed by the flame but never be in direct contact with it.

BANANA BOATS

This is an inventive variation on a classic campfire s'more. Using a whole banana as the cooking vessel, this dish is as fun and easy to consume as it is to prepare. The gooey marshmallows, melted chocolate, and toasted graham crackers combine with baked banana and smoky fire essence for the perfect campfire treat. When you're camping, convenience is king, and being able to produce a quick-and-easy dessert while you're fireside is what it's all about.

4 semi-ripe bananas

4oz (110g) milk chocolate

4 graham crackers

1 cup (60g) mini marshmallows

1 Begin by preparing your heat source. You'll need a fire or an oven preheated to 350°F (180°C).

2 Slice a lengthwise incision into each banana, following the inner curve and keeping the peel on. This will help prevent the toppings from falling out.

3 Using your thumb, lightly press the banana flat from top to bottom, widening the slit.

4 On one side, arrange pieces of chocolate. On the other side, arrange pieces of graham cracker. Sprinkle marshmallows down the center.

5 Wrap the banana tightly with foil. Place the foil-wrapped bananas around the campfire, away from direct heat. You want to bake them, not burn them. Keep the toppings facing up at all times to prevent making a mess.

6 When marshmallows become gooey, you are ready to unwrap and enjoy.

If cooking these by a fire, it's a good idea to use the perimeter of the pit, taking your time with it, to prevent them from getting too hot. Burnt chocolate doesn't taste very good, so rotate them often, making sure to keep them upright.

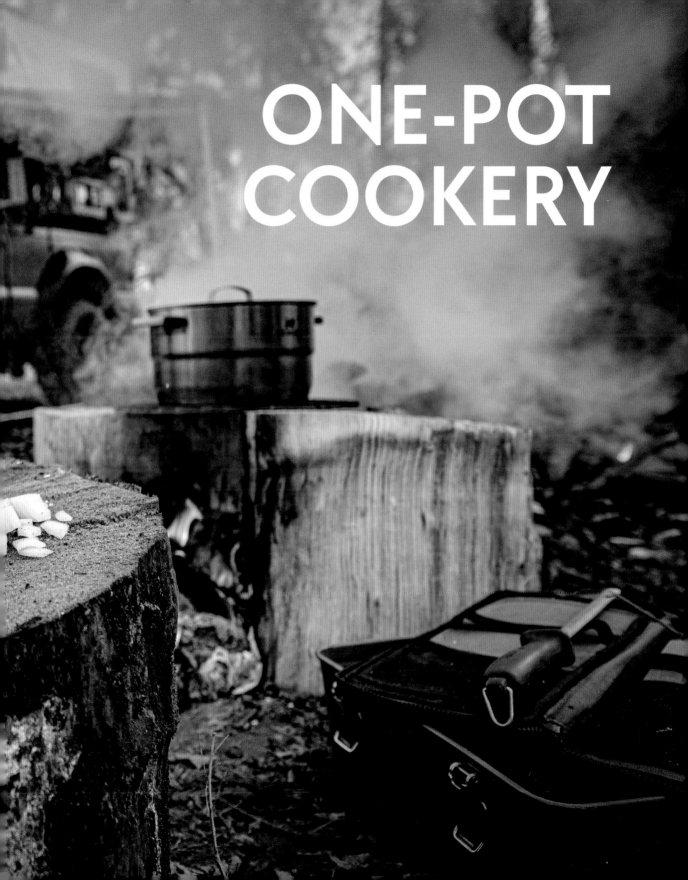

ONE-POT
COOKERY

Cooking with one pot is one of the main chapters I wanted to include in this book. While it's incredibly convenient to have every tool and gadget under the sun, knowing how to cook with just one pot ultimately proves how well you know how to cook. By cooking with one pot, not only do you save space and time, you also layer and create flavors that simply can't be done any other way. There is a simplicity and elegance to creating a dish from one vessel.

The most important thing to remember when attempting to cook with one pot is to adhere to an order of operations. We cook the most resilient foods first to extract flavor and caramelize natural sugars in the ingredients. Once you accomplish this caramelization with one ingredient, you move on to the next, ultimately gaining as much flavor as possible, all while keeping these flavors contained in just one vessel. In most cases, this means you'll eventually be deglazing using some sort of liquid, whether that's beer, stock, cream, wine, or just water. Once all your ingredients have become crisp at the bottom of the pan, it's the deglazing process (when you add liquid and scrape the bottom of the pan) that releases all of the delicious flavors that makes one-pot cookery what it is.

When I think of our ancestors cooking, I think of them using fire and one pot. This sort of witch's cauldron technique has always been full of opportunities, creating countless recipes worldwide. It's no secret that one-pot cookery is the original form of cooking. In the past, we didn't have a plethora of pots and pans to choose from. We just had the one pot and our creativity to guide us.

Cooking with just one pot allows you to layer ingredients and create complex flavors that can't be made any other way.

For more obvious reasons, the one-pot approach to cooking just makes life easier. When I was cooking in small spaces professionally, I found these one-pot dishes to be time-savers and crowd-pleasers. I could do a minimal amount of prep work, throw it all in a pot, and only have to worry about managing the temperature. We're simply prepping ingredients and focusing our efforts into one pot, aiming to extract as much flavor as we possibly can from the ingredients. With one pot, you can continuously add ingredients and manage your dish's flavor to your liking. If it needs a little more salt, you can add it. If it needs a little more cream, you can add it. Just remember you can always add more, but you can't take it away.

One-pot cookery also saves you time by limiting the amount of effort and cleanup required. Often when cooking, people like to reach for another dish when it's really not necessary. When preparing one-pot recipes in this chapter, like the Jambalaya, instead of grabbing another vessel, I choose to push the meat to the back or corner of the pot, creating a cold zone for the cooked items and leaving a hot clear area to caramelize the next ingredient. Rather than removing those items, dirtying another dish, and placing it back into the pan, you can truly just use the one pot.

Another good example is the Mac & Cheese recipe. You can drain the water from the pot (without removing the noodles or dirtying another dish). If the pot has a lid, then you have a strainer. The same goes for the Beef & Lasagna Stew. Why boil water and create a flavorless pasta in it? You can just as easily cook that pasta in a flavorful sauce and allow it to soak up all that deliciousness instead. One-pot cookery saves you effort, space, fuel, time, water, and cleanup. It just makes sense to cook more recipes with only one pot, and this chapter provides the recipes to help you get started.

SHAKSHUKA

Eating a meal without utensils became a practice I learned about while living in Kuwait City and during my travels to countries in North Africa. A lot of traditional meals in these regions are consumed by using your hands and a piece of bread that works in place of a utensil. These breads are used to scoop rice, meat, vegetables, curries, and sauces. Western cultures commonly refrain from the act of eating without a utensil, but I find this to be somewhat of a travesty. For those of us living minimally, not needing to use a utensil makes a whole lot of sense. You can create meals that use fewer dishes and that also don't require utensils, all while providing for a more novel eating experience. This recipe is the perfect example of a delicious meal that's made in one pot and consumed without traditional utensils.

3 tbsp olive oil

1 small white onion, diced

1 green bell pepper, julienned

2 garlic cloves, minced

5 Roma tomatoes, diced

2 tsp salt

1 tsp pepper

4 eggs

¼ cup (40g) crumbled feta, to garnish

3–4 sprigs basil, to garnish

4 slices sourdough bread or one baguette

1 Begin by preparing your heat source. You'll need a fire or a stovetop burner set at medium heat.

2 Heat the olive oil in a high-walled saucepan over medium heat.

3 Add the onion and bell pepper and cook until translucent. This should take about 5 minutes.

4 Add the garlic, tomatoes, salt, and pepper. Let simmer on low heat for 10 minutes.

5 Crack the eggs directly into the sauce. Try your best to not break the yolk. Cover with a lid or foil and cook for about 4 minutes more or until the eggs are over easy.

6 Garnish the completed dish right in the saucepan with feta and basil, and serve with toasted bread.

When preparing eggs to your favorite doneness, I find it's best to keep a close eye on the egg whites. The longest part of egg cookery is getting the whites cooked where they meet the yolk. Once this has been accomplished, the yolk itself will cook relatively fast. So if you enjoy nice runny egg yolks to dip your bread into, keep a very close eye on the egg whites, because one minute after they're cooked, so are the yolks.

QUESO FUNDIDO

Queso is a holiday staple in my family. We don't celebrate a birthday or any major holiday without making some type of queso. I prefer to use Mexican-style beef chorizo over the Spanish sausage-style chorizo. It adds more fat, color, and depth of flavor. This dish feeds many people, leaving everyone feeling satisfied with very little cleanup. Communal campfire meals like this are what it's all about. It's a beautiful moment to sit around the fire with everyone reaching in to get a big scoop of queso with their chips. This dish also works great as an accoutrement to tacos, enchiladas, Spanish rice, and virtually any type of Latin food. You could even put it on top of a cheeseburger or a hot dog as a delicious condiment.

12oz (340g) beef chorizo

1 jalapeño, diced

1 bunch green onions, sliced, white and green parts separated

2 cups (200g) grated quesadilla cheese or whole-milk Jack cheese

Tortilla chips, to serve

1 Begin by preparing your heat source. You'll need a fire, a grill, or a stovetop burner set at medium heat.

2 Place a medium cast-iron skillet over medium heat. When hot, add the chorizo and cook, stirring occasionally, for 10 minutes. The chorizo will liquefy and excess liquid will cook off. The objective is to fry the meat in its own fat.

3 Once the fat is fully rendered, use a spoon to hold back the meat and drain off the excess fat. Reserve 2 to 3 tablespoons cooked chorizo for garnish.

4 Add the jalapeño and the whites of the onion to the pan with the chorizo. Cook for 2 minutes.

5 Fold in the shredded cheese with the chorizo. Continue stirring while the cheese melts.

6 Once the cheese is fully melted, reduce the heat and keep warm. Garnish with the reserved chorizo and the green parts of the onion.

7 Serve with tortilla chips or in a taco!

This dish works with any type of melty cheese. Don't feel like you have to use quesadilla cheese if you can't find it in your local store.

WHITE BEAN & BACON STEW

The beauty of cooking with only one pot is that it forces you to employ the art of layering flavors. In this dish, you start with the bacon, add the onions, and deglaze all the caramelized bits from the bottom, yielding layered flavors. A dish like this simple stew perfectly encapsulates the meaning of building flavor.

1lb (450g) bacon, diced

1 white or yellow onion, diced

2 ribs celery, diced

3 garlic cloves, minced

1 carrot, grated

4 large kale leaves, stems removed, chopped

1 (15.5oz/439g) can white beans (any variety)

1qt (1L) chicken stock

Salt and pepper, to taste

Fresh rosemary and/or parsley, to garnish

Bread, to serve

1 Begin by preparing your heat source. You'll need a fire or a stovetop burner set at medium-high heat.

2 In a large, deep skillet or pot, cook the bacon for 10 minutes or until golden brown.

3 Add the onion, celery, and garlic, and sauté for 10 to 15 minutes or until the onion is translucent.

4 Stir in the carrot, kale, and white beans. Add the chicken stock, and simmer for 30 minutes or until the kale is tender.

5 Taste and season with salt and pepper. Cool for 10 to 20 minutes before serving with the fresh herbs and bread.

ONE-POT COOKERY 147

Cooking a complete dish in one pot elevates your food's complexity—and it just tastes better. Use one pot as often as possible to pack your dishes full of layered flavor.

CHUCK STEAK CHILI

When I was growing up, we ate chili almost weekly, and it's become a nostalgic dish in my life. What makes a great chili, or any stew for that matter, is the layering of flavor. This typically begins with a hard sear of the protein—in this case, beef chuck—which develops a rich and sweet addition to the base of your pot. By deglazing that caramelized flavor, you enrich the dish as you continue to add more ingredients. This dish is best served with cornbread, sour cream, cheddar cheese, and a little green onion to garnish.

1 tbsp olive oil

2lb (1kg) beef chuck roast

1 tbsp salt, plus more to taste

1 white onion, diced

2 ribs celery, diced

1 large carrot, grated

1 (15oz/425g) can tomato purée

3oz (85g) tomato paste

1 bay leaf

3 tbsp chili powder

1 tbsp ground cumin

1 tbsp red pepper flakes

2 cups (475ml) beef broth

2 (15.5oz/439g) cans chili or kidney beans

1 Begin by preparing your heat source. You'll need a fire or a stovetop burner set at medium-high heat.

2 In a large stockpot over medium-high heat, heat the olive oil. Evenly coat the roast on all sides with salt and place in the pot. Sear on both sides until golden brown, about 5 minutes per side. Remove from the pan and set aside.

3 To the pot, add the onion, celery, and carrot. Sauté over medium-high heat for 5 minutes or until translucent. Be sure to scrape up all the beef bits from the bottom of the pot.

4 Add the tomato purée, tomato paste, bay leaf, chili powder, cumin, and red pepper flakes. Stir thoroughly. Add the beef broth to the pot along with the chuck roast.

5 Cover and simmer on low for up to 3 hours or until the chuck steak is fork-tender. (The total cooking time will depend on the thickness of the beef.)

6 Remove the meat and let cool for 10 minutes or until it is cool enough to handle. Shred the meat and return it to the pot. Stir in the beans and let simmer for 10 to 15 minutes more. Remove the bay leaf. Taste and adjust the seasoning as needed. Serve warm.

Chili freezes incredibly well, and only gets better with age, so make this in advance and bring it with you on your next adventure.

JAMBALAYA

I was surrounded by a lot of Southern and Cajun-inspired cuisine growing up. Dishes like gumbo, shrimp étouffée, hush puppies, grits, and, of course, jambalaya, were frequently on the table. I often refer to jambalaya as the American version of paella, and I believe most cultures around the world have some form of this one-pot meal, full of meat, rice, and local vegetables. I love jambalaya for its big flavors and meaty textures. Recipes like this are fantastic for small kitchens, being outdoors, and traveling, because all the flavor is developed within one pot, eliminating the need to dirty a bunch of dishes.

2 tbsp olive oil

1 boneless, skinless chicken breast

1½ tsp salt, divided

1½ tsp black pepper, divided

8oz (225g) shrimp, peeled and deveined

8oz (225g) andouille sausage, diced

½ yellow onion, diced

2 ribs celery, diced

2 garlic cloves, minced

½ green bell pepper, diced

½ red bell pepper

1 jalapeño, diced

2 tbsp Cajun seasoning

1 bay leaf

8oz (225g) crushed tomatoes

2½ cups (600ml) chicken stock

1 cup (190g) medium-grain white rice

Thyme leaves, to garnish

1 Begin by preparing your heat source. You'll need a fire or a stovetop burner set at medium-high heat.

2 In a large, high-sided skillet with a lid, heat the oil over medium-high heat. Lightly coat the chicken with about ½ teaspoon each of the salt and the pepper. Add the chicken to the pan and sear on both sides until golden brown, 5 to 10 minutes per side until fully cooked. Remove and set aside.

3 Pat the shrimp dry, and sear in the same pan over medium-high heat until golden brown on both sides, about 2 minutes per side. You can add additional oil if needed. Lightly season with salt and pepper while cooking. Remove the shrimp from the pan and set aside with the chicken.

4 Add the andouille sausage to the pan and cook, stirring occasionally, for 5 to 10 minutes. The objective is to get a hard caramelization. You want to see a dark, caramelized layer on each sausage slice.

5 Reduce the heat to medium, and add the onion, celery, garlic, bell peppers, and jalapeño to the pan. Cook for 10 minutes, stirring occasionally, until the onion and celery are translucent. Be sure to scrape up all of the good flavors from the bottom of the pan from searing the meat.

6 Mix in the Cajun seasoning, remaining 1 teaspoon salt and black pepper, bay leaf, crushed tomatoes, and chicken stock. Stir and bring to a boil.

7 Sprinkle the rice evenly around the pan. Using a fork, make sure all the rice is submerged and evenly distributed. Reduce the heat to low, cover, and cook for 15 to 20 minutes or until the rice is fully cooked.

8 Meanwhile, dice the chicken and shrimp. Once the rice is fully cooked, add the chicken and shrimp to the pot and lightly mix together. Do not overmix.

9 Remove the bay leaf and serve immediately, garnished with the thyme.

ONE-POT COOKERY 153

Jambalaya is a dish that can be made with a variety of ingredients. If you're ever in a pinch for what to cook, this recipe can be modified to utilize whatever you already have sitting around.

MAC & CHEESE

By using residual heat from the pot cooking the pasta, and the heat of the pasta itself, we're able to eliminate the need to make the cheese sauce in advance. In addition, we no longer need a strainer or an extra sauce pot—just the one pot will do. Use a lid or variety of different tools like a simple chef's knife to hold the pasta back while you drain the water. You can boil the pasta, make the sauce, and create a broiled served dish, all in the same pan. You could even cook ham or bacon in the base prior to adding the water to cook the pasta, adding yet another layer of flavor.

Salt, to taste

1lb (450g) macaroni or other short pasta shape

1 cup (240g) heavy whipping cream

2 cups (240g) grated Havarti cheese

2 cups (200g) grated Gruyère cheese

Pepper, to taste

1 Begin by preparing your heat source. You'll need a fire, a grill, or a stovetop burner set at high heat.

2 Pour the appropriate amount of water for your pasta (according to the package instructions) into a large pot. Add salt to the water until it tastes like the ocean. Bring the water to a boil and add in the pasta.

3 When the pasta is cooked but still firm to the bite, strain the water from the pot using a lid or a chef's knife to hold back the pasta.

4 Add the cream and cheeses. Reheat over medium heat, mixing constantly until the pasta is fully cooked through and the cheese sauce has formed.

5 Add salt and pepper to taste. Serve warm.

For even more flavor, cook diced ham or bacon in the pot before adding water to boil the pasta.

BEEF & LASAGNA STEW

This hearty beef and tomato stew relies on a technique of cooking pasta directly in a sauce that's nothing revolutionary. It seems like common sense because the pasta will absorb flavors, right? Why would we want to cook it in plain water when it could soak up the flavorful sauce? Those days are numbered. From now on, try letting your pasta spend more time cooking in sauces. The beauty, of course, is that there will only be one dish to clean.

2–3 tbsp olive oil

1lb (450g) ground beef

½ yellow onion, diced

1 carrot, grated

2 garlic cloves, minced

6oz (170g) can tomato paste

1 (15oz/425g) can crushed tomatoes

3 cups (710ml) beef broth

Salt and pepper, to taste

5–6 lasagna noodles

Parmesan cheese, freshly grated, to garnish

Basil leaves, to garnish

1 Begin by preparing your heat source. You'll need a fire or a stovetop burner set at medium-high heat.

2 In a large pot, heat the olive oil over the heat source. Add the ground beef and cook, breaking up the meat with a spoon, for 5 to 6 minutes or until browned.

3 Stir in the onion, carrot, and garlic. Cook for 10 minutes more.

4 Stir in the tomato paste, mixing well. Add the crushed tomatoes and beef broth. Season with salt and pepper to taste, and simmer for 10 minutes.

5 Using your hands, break the lasagna noodles in half, and gently add them one at a time to the simmering sauce. Try to prevent the pasta from stacking on top of itself.

6 Cover and cook over medium-low heat for 30 to 45 minutes or until the noodles are fully cooked and the sauce has thickened. If the sauce becomes too thick before the noodles are cooked, add water ¼ cup (60ml) at a time. (You can always add water, but you can't take it away!)

7 Serve hot, topped with the Parmesan cheese and basil.

You can use the technique of cooking pasta in sauce for just about all forms of pasta cookery. In Italy, the pasta is often left undercooked before entering the sauce for its final minutes of cooking. This allows the pasta to fully absorb the flavors of the dish.

BAKED BRIE
WITH BLUEBERRIES & PECANS

This simple dish of warm brie with berries, nuts, and honey scooped onto toasted bread is sure to please your friends and family. It makes a quick-and-easy appetizer or lunch at camp. The ease of preparation means you'll have more free time to relax and enjoy the outdoors. Simply warm the cheese long enough for the berries to pop and enjoy.

1 (8oz/225g) wheel of brie

2 cups (380g) fresh blueberries

½ cup (50g) pecans

Pinch of salt

Sliced bread of choice, to serve

2 tbsp honey, to garnish

1 Begin by preparing your heat source. You'll need a fire, a grill, or an oven preheated to 400°F (200°C).

2 Using a knife, score the top of the cheese in a cross-hatch pattern to a depth of ¼ inch (6mm). Place the cheese in the center of a cast-iron skillet.

3 Add the blueberries, pecans, and salt to the pan, distributing them evenly around the cheese. Place on the grill or in the oven and cook for about 15 minutes.

4 Meanwhile, toast your bread either by placing slices directly on the grill over low heat or using a toaster oven.

5 When the berries have popped and the cheese is melting, you're ready to go. Broil for a few minutes to give it a nice, blackened top. Drizzle with honey, dip your fresh bread, and enjoy.

Try other combinations of berries and nuts. Baked brie is delicious with blackberries or raspberries, and feel free to use walnuts, hazelnuts, or almonds.

ON THE WATER

I've been a professional chef for fifteen years, and ten of those years have been spent cooking out on the open ocean. When I began cooking professionally in my early twenties, I had no idea that I'd eventually end up out at sea. I had very little experience on boats at first, as the only boat I'd ever been on was my grandpa's little sailboat out in San Francisco Bay. I did, however, have an extreme love for the ocean as an avid surfer.

My time as a chef on the water started after I graduated from culinary school in San Diego when I got an email about an open position for a chef on a yacht. I literally quit my job that very same day and applied for this position, with no guarantee that I'd actually get the job. About a week later, I was interviewing with the owner of a super yacht at the local harbor in San Diego, surrounded by boats. Luckily, I got the job. This was the beginning of what would become a career as a chef on the high seas.

With no experience cooking on boats, I flew off to Vancouver, Canada, where I took my first steps on a massive super yacht. The boat was dry docked when I arrived. It was here where I met the crew for the first time. We remained dry docked for about a week, anticipating the boat's departure and release into the water. I truly had no idea what I'd gotten myself into. Eventually, we set sail, and it was time for me to prove that I had what it takes to cook while under way. Within hours of being out to sea, I found myself cradling the toilet, totally seasick, and

thinking there was no way I was going to be able to cook dinner. And I didn't. The owner of the yacht made himself a tuna sandwich instead. Thankfully he was an understanding guy, but my seasickness didn't go away. It continued for the duration of the trip up to Alaska. Turns out, I was not seaworthy.

Despite my tough introduction to cooking at sea, I stuck it out—trip after trip, port after port, looking out my galley window trying to gain some relief from staring down at my cutting board. Over time, this got easier and easier, and eventually, I got rolled out of my bunk enough times that I forgot what seasickness even was.

The majority of the 100,000+ nautical miles I sailed took place in Pacific waters, from Alaska to Mexico, Hawaii, and Australia. These are notoriously some of the roughest seas in the world. Needless to say, cooking in these conditions can be a challenge. After a lot of time spent on the Pacific, I found myself cooking on the East Coast of the Americas, from Newfoundland to Puerto Rico, and then all around the Mediterranean Sea in Europe. I remember thinking to myself, *These waters are so much easier. Are we even sailing?* After having done so much work on the relentless Pacific Ocean, everything else felt like child's play. At the end of the day, cooking in difficult environments can help equip you to cook literally anywhere, under any circumstances.

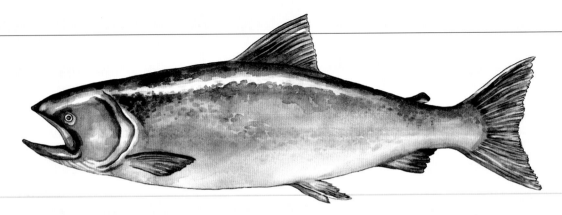

How to fillet a fish

the Adventure Chef Way

---

1. Be sure you have a good, <u>sharp</u> knife to use and a flat, stable surface.

---

2. If you're right-handed, grasp the fish head by the gill plate with your left hand.

Using your right hand, place your knife under the fin next to the gill plate.

---

3. Push the knife through the flesh parallel to the bones. Pull with your left hand on the head to provide additional force.

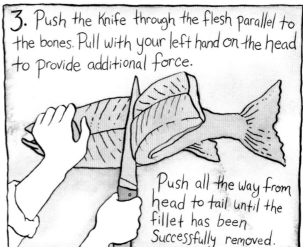

Push all the way from head to tail until the fillet has been successfully removed.

---

4. Flip the fish over and repeat. Remove any pin bones with tweezers, or don't - I often just leave them in, they remove easily when the fish is cooked.

---

5. Trim any excess fats, bloodline, skin, etc. For smaller fish (like trout) keep as whole fillets and cook with the skin on.

For larger fish, portion into fist-sized pieces.

Preparing recipes on (or near) the water is a chapter in this book for two main reasons. One, it's the place where I became a professional and made so many memories over the years. The water is and will forever be a massive part of my identity. Two, the lessons I learned while preparing great dishes on boats will apply to anyone attempting to produce good food in a small space with limited supplies. The knowledge of cooking in a galley is what this book is all about, and it all stems from my life at sea.

One of my favorite sea stories is when I cooked for an old cowboy named Rick. This guy is a legend. He wore a Rolex attached to a pewter wristband with turquoise insets. With his big handlebar mustache, he would swallow his dip because he claimed it would be "unsanitary" to spit in the galley. Rick had been cooking on boats probably since before I was born, and had a lot of wisdom to share with me. You see, he was basically the only executive chef I'd ever had. I was there to replace him. He was getting too old for the job, so he took it upon himself to teach me everything he knew about cooking at sea. When I first arrived, I had it in my head from culinary school that you're only allowed to use dry towels because a wet towel will burn you. Turns out, on boats, you mostly want wet towels. Rick was the first person to insist I work on top of wet towels, for everything. He taught me how to make a ring with a wet towel to place my vegetables in the middle of it on the counter so they wouldn't roll off due to the rocking waves. This wet towel trick saved countless prepped items, breads, desserts, sauces, and plates from hitting the floor while under way, and it was the simplest piece of advice from an old cowboy.

When you're cooking in a small galley kitchen on a boat, you have to learn how to manage the space effectively to prevent spills and disasters from happening in the cupboards or the refrigerator. We often placed rolled-up towels in these spaces to prevent items from moving around, paired with a hair tie to keep the doors from opening on their own. I also found that keeping the cupboards full of quality ingredients made it so they couldn't shift around, while also ensuring that I had an ample supply of goods while out at sea.

CEVICHE

Ceviche is a recipe born on the water. It highlights the act of catching a fresh fish and eating it in minutes—something that's always appealed to me. The freshness and well-rounded nature of ceviche is exactly how fish was intended to be consumed: with very few ingredients and without cooking the fish. The acidity denatures the protein, changing its color and texture, and brings about a different flavor experience than cooking the fish does.

1lb (450g) white seafood (cod, snapper, halibut, shrimp, etc.), cut into small ½-inch (1.25cm) chunks

1¼ cups (300ml) freshly squeezed lime juice (from 10–15 limes)

1 mango, diced

1 serrano pepper, diced

½ red onion, diced

1 Roma tomato, diced

½ English cucumber, diced

1 bunch cilantro, leaves only, chopped

Salt and pepper, to taste

TO SERVE:

Tortilla chips

Sliced avocado

Tajin seasoning or hot sauce

1 In a large nonmetal bowl or zip-top freezer bag, combine the seafood and lime juice. Gently mix to ensure that the fish is covered completely by the juice. Cover and refrigerate for 30 minutes.

2 Remove the seafood from the fridge. It should now be opaque rather than translucent. Add the mango, serrano pepper, red onion, tomato, cucumber, and cilantro. Gently mix to combine. Season with salt and pepper to taste. Cover and return to the refrigerator for 30 minutes for the flavors to meld.

3 Serve with fresh tortilla chips and sliced avocado. For added heat, sprinkle with Tajin or hot sauce.

Ingredients used for ceviche vary from region to region. My favorite variation of ceviche comes from Fiji, where coconut and coconut milk are major components of the dish. I like this variation because it's less common to have a dish that's creamy as well as spicy and acidic.
To make this version, add half a can of coconut milk to this recipe.
(I generally avoid adding a lot of the fatty cream on top—just the watery milk below is good.)

TUNA POKE SALAD

I was introduced to this poke recipe when I was sailing from San Diego, California, to Sydney, Australia. About halfway across the Pacific Ocean, I found myself in Hawaii, where the poke is to die for. Poke was created in Polynesia to help fishermen extend the longevity of their catch, as coating the cubes of raw fish with chili, salt, soy, and oil helps to preserve it.

1½lb (680g) ahi tuna (frozen is okay; fresh is better)

1 shallot, thinly sliced

1 tbsp fresh ginger, minced

1 tbsp sesame seeds

2 tbsp sambal (chili paste)

3 tbsp soy sauce

2 tbsp sesame oil

2 tbsp coarse sea salt, plus more for sprinkling

1 tbsp cracked black pepper

1 cup (240ml) cooking oil, for frying

3–4 wonton wrappers, rolled and thinly sliced

1–2 slices avocado, to serve

4 green onions, sliced, to garnish

1 Cut the tuna into cubes of equal size and place in a large bowl. (If using frozen tuna, don't fully thaw before slicing; using partially frozen tuna makes it easier to cut into cubes and maintains nice clean edges.)

2 To the bowl, add the shallot, ginger, sesame seeds, sambal, soy sauce, sesame oil, sea salt, and pepper. Gently mix, taking care not to damage the cubes of fish. Refrigerate (or store in a cooler) while you prepare the fried wontons.

3 Prepare your heat source. You'll need a fire or a stovetop burner set at medium-high heat.

4 In a small pan, heat the oil over medium-high heat to 350°F (180°C). Carefully add the julienned wonton wrappers to the hot oil and fry until just golden brown, about 20 seconds. Using a kitchen spider or slotted spoon, remove and transfer to paper towels to drain. Immediately season with salt.

5 Serve the chilled poke salad with the avocado slices and crispy wontons, and garnish with the green onions.

ON THE WATER 169

Poke is an excellent way to utilize the cuts of your whole fresh catch of tuna that aren't suitable to serve as steaks or sashimi—100 percent utilization.

MUSSELS
WITH WHITE WINE DIPPING BROTH

Steamed mussels and a good baguette rank high as one of the all-time easiest and most delicious meals. With just a few simple and common ingredients, and a few minutes of your time, you'll be able to create something elegant and tasty. Steam mussels in a buttery white wine and garlic-infused dipping sauce. Toast off a good baguette and dig right in. The beautiful thing about this dish is how little time you'll use, and how few dishes you'll create in the process. This recipe does very well over a campfire, too—such a simple way of cooking in one pot.

8 tbsp butter

6 garlic cloves, thinly sliced

3lb (1.4kg) mussels (in shell)

½ cup (120ml) white wine

1 tsp black pepper

½ cup (12g) chopped parsley, to garnish

1 crusty baguette, to serve

1 Begin by preparing your heat source. You'll need a fire or a stovetop burner set at medium heat.

2 In a large stockpot, melt the butter. Add the garlic and cook for 2 to 3 minutes.

3 Add the cleaned mussels to the pot and deglaze with the white wine. Add the pepper and stir thoroughly.

4 Cover with a lid. Let the mussels steam just long enough for all of them to open, 10 to 15 minutes.

5 Garnish the mussels and broth with the parsley.

6 Toast the baguette and dip in the broth to enjoy with the mussels.

Mussels can be found on shorelines around the world, including both the East and West Coasts of the United States. Look for them on beaches at low tide, growing in clumps attached to large rocks or dock pilings. If you see them, don't be afraid to grab a few handfuls and prepare this recipe. Before doing so, however, be sure to obtain a shellfish license (if required in that area) and check the local biotoxin levels to ensure safe consumption. When harvesting wild mussels, be sure to remove the beard—the stringy, fibrous material that anchors the mussel to the object on which it grows. It should be removed prior to consumption. To do so, firmly hold the mussel in one hand while pinching the beard with the other. Push and pull simultaneously in an upward motion, and the beard should dislodge from the mussel.

ROGUE RIVER ROLL

Smoked fish salad is a versatile and portable meal whether you're on the road or on the water. It makes a delicious sandwich stuffed into a po' boy roll and topped with lettuce and tomato, but you can also simply bring along some fresh bread or crackers or eat it over a bed of leafy greens. The mayonnaise and lemon combined with the smoked nature of the meat will help prolong the shelf life of this dish.

8oz (225g) smoked salmon or trout

Zest and juice of 1 lemon

2 tbsp mayonnaise

Salt and pepper, to taste

1 bunch dill, minced

½ red onion, finely diced

1 rib celery, finely diced

4 po' boy rolls (split top) or hot dog buns

Lettuce and sliced tomato (optional), to serve

1 Using your hands, break up the fish into bite-sized chunks, removing the skin and any bones. Place in a medium bowl.

2 In a small bowl, combine the lemon zest, lemon juice, mayonnaise, a pinch of salt, and a pinch of pepper.

3 To the bowl with the salmon, add the dill, onion, and celery. Add the lemon-mayo mixture and gently mix until just combined.

4 Scoop the smoked salmon mixture into the rolls (feel free to toast them), top with the lettuce and tomato, add a fresh squeeze of lemon juice, and enjoy!

This recipe can be made with any type of smoked fish, so don't be afraid to use something other than salmon or trout. Try it with smoked marlin or swordfish.

CRISPY SHRIMP PATTIES

This is more than just a simple shrimp recipe; this recipe applies to just about all types of seafood. The act of mincing and binding the seafood with egg and cornstarch is all we're doing. You can play with the ingredients, but I find the ginger-garlic-green-onion combo to pair well with seafood. The cornstarch will provide that classic Asian-style crunch, and the egg will help hold it all together.

1lb (450g) medium shrimp, peeled, deveined, and minced

¼ cup (30g) finely diced ginger

2 garlic cloves, minced

½ cup (50g) finely diced green onions, plus more to garnish

1 large egg

½ cup (65g) cornstarch

Pinch of salt and pepper

½ cup (120ml) peanut oil

Sesame seeds (optional), to garnish

1 Begin by preparing your heat source. You'll need a fire or a stovetop burner set at medium-high heat.

2 To a large bowl, add the shrimp, ginger, garlic, and green onions. Mix to combine.

3 Add the egg to the shrimp mixture and combine thoroughly.

4 Add the cornstarch, salt, and pepper, and combine until the mixture firms up slightly.

5 Add the peanut oil to a cast-iron pan over medium-high heat.

6 Using a wet spoon, scoop a portion of the shrimp mixture into the pan and flatten it with the back of the spoon. The patty should be about ½ inch (1.25cm) thick.

7 Fry on one side for about 5 minutes or until golden brown. Flip and repeat.

8 Remove each patty from the oil, and sprinkle with sesame seeds, salt, and more green onions to garnish. Ponzu, tamari, and soy all make great dipping sauces for this if you have any of them!

You could also use this recipe to create a delicious po' boy sandwich filling, which makes this easier to eat on the go.

CRAB
WITH COCONUT CURRY BROTH

People often steam crab or dip it in butter with lemon. But what if we tried something different? What if we tried something lively and packed full of Pacific Island flavors? I love crab, and after years of cooking it all over the world, I find this recipe to be my favorite. Garlic, ginger, and onion fried with curry paste and coconut milk makes a quick, flavorful broth, and steaming the crab shells in the broth infuses it with crab essence. Make this and you'll have everyone crowding around the pot, asking what smells so delicious.

1 tbsp coconut oil (olive oil, sesame oil, or vegetable oil will also do)

¼ cup (30g) finely diced ginger

1 serrano pepper, finely diced

5 garlic cloves

½ red onion, thinly sliced

1 tbsp red curry paste

1 (13.5oz/400ml) can coconut milk

1 red bell pepper, finely diced

2 limes

2⅕lb (1kg) Dungeness crab legs (any crab will work), thawed if frozen

Cilantro leaves, to garnish

Cooked white rice (optional), to serve

1 Begin by preparing your heat source. You'll need a fire or a stovetop burner set at medium heat.

2 In a large stockpot, heat the coconut oil. Add the ginger, serrano pepper, garlic, and red onion and cook for no more than 1 minute. Take care not to burn. Stir in the red curry paste and mix thoroughly.

3 Add the coconut milk, red bell pepper, and the zest and juice of 1 lime. Bring to a boil, then reduce to low heat.

4 Add the crab legs to the pot and cover with a lid. Steam for 8 to 10 minutes. The crab is completely cooked through when the leg meat is no longer opaque or clear, but rather solid white with pink specks.

5 Once the crab is fully cooked, transfer the individual legs to bowls, and spoon the coconut curry broth over the top, completely coating the legs.

6 Garnish with the cilantro and the juice from the remaining lime, and dip your crab meat in the broth as you consume the legs. Serve with a bowl of rice, if desired.

Make this broth with any type of protein—chicken, fish, and even beef are all excellent choices. If using another type of seafood or meat, add some bouillon to boost the flavor of the broth. Crab is abundant all around the world, and it's easy for beginners and amateurs to learn how to catch and harvest it themselves. If you're near any northern ocean, it's worth the investment to get yourself a crab trap and a license, walk out to the local dock, and attempt to harvest some yourself.

BROILED BLACK COD
WITH MISO GLAZE

With this simple technique, fish cooks quickly under the high heat of the broiler. The miso-based glaze is a perfect complement to the buttery, flaky flesh of black cod. However, black cod is often difficult to find, so don't feel obligated to buy it. You'll be pleasantly surprised to find that this same cooking method works beautifully for a variety of fish.

2 tbsp red miso paste

1 tbsp rice vinegar

1 tbsp shoyu

2 tbsp soy sauce

1 tbsp olive oil, for the pan

4 black cod fillets, about 8oz (225g) each

1   Begin by preparing your heat source. Preheat a pizza oven to 550°F (290°C) or adjust the top oven rack to sit about 8 inches (20cm) below the broiler.

2   In a small saucepan, combine the red miso paste, rice vinegar, shoyu, and soy sauce. Bring to a simmer over medium heat. Whisk until the miso paste has dissolved and the mixture has thickened. Remove from the heat.

3   Line a rimmed baking sheet with foil and coat it with the olive oil. Place the fish fillets on the prepared pan, skin side down. Brush the miso glaze over the fillets, coating them liberally. Reserve a little bit of the glaze to apply during cooking.

4   Place the pan in the preheated pizza oven or under the broiler. Cook for about 5 minutes, brushing the fish with additional miso glaze halfway through cooking, until the glaze has caramelized and the fish flakes easily with a fork. (Cook times will vary depending on the thickness of the fish.)

Try this recipe with fresh salmon, grouper, or trout—just about any fish accepts these flavors incredibly well.

IN A SMALL SPACE

After more than a decade of cooking professionally in a space the size of some people's closets, I learned a few things about preparing food in small spaces. These skills are fairly niche, but they apply directly to the kind of life I've been living—from boats, to campers and vans, to eventually a tiny house. The lessons and techniques I've learned along the way have made my life easier and my time spent cooking more enjoyable. They have also made me a better chef.

Over the years, I've found ways to eliminate the need to use lots of dishes, and instead I cook in a manner that's easy for me to clean up. Most people dislike doing the dishes, and sometimes it even deters them from wanting to cook in the first place. Well, what if we made less mess?

With less cleanup time, we've freed up our time to be more creative when we cook, more encouraged to try new things, have fun, and enjoy the experience of making a delicious meal. In a small space, it can be a challenge to keep things neat and tidy, but there are several ways to keep your cooking area clean:

- Organize your ingredients and tools in ways that make them easily findable and accessible.

- Since gadgets take up space, if you don't regularly use a kitchen tool, get rid of it.

- When space is limited, stack up prepped goods instead of letting them spread out.

- When you're done using a dish or tool, clean it, dry it, and put it away.

- Clean as you go, so the number of dishes and tools to clean at the end doesn't feel daunting.

- Be conscious of how you use your space, not creating too many recipes at once.

Believe it or not, you can create incredible meals with limited ingredients in all kinds of small spaces.

Galley kitchens, whether big or small, inside or outside, are generally less spacious and require creating an efficient cooking area that will equip you for success. Galley-style cooking works best when your space is well organized and kept clean. There are several ways to keep your ingredients and food products organized, which will set you up for success cooking in small spaces. Some of the important ones include the following:

- Make items in advance whenever possible and only pull them out when you need them.

- Room temperature is your best friend if you have limited space in the fridge.

- Be aware of how much food you need versus how much you're about to make.

- Only keep leftovers for as long as they're good to eat, and toss them when they've gotten old.

- Cook recipes that use fewer ingredients; they require less prep, time, and space.

- Find ways to cook with one pot/pan/cookie sheet. Don't feel like each ingredient needs to have its own vessel.

Often, I've found that the best recipes require the fewest ingredients. These kinds of dishes are often simple, but also special, since the person enjoying the meal knows exactly what they're eating and can taste each ingredient in every bite. Simplicity works well in a small space and should be kept in mind whenever cooking where space is limited.

When you have a good sense of what your cooking style is, you can keep the equipment you have on hand to a minimum. Getting creative with the tools you do have can often lead to pleasantly surprising results. You don't need much to put together a great meal.

The recipes in this chapter, and really the whole book for that matter, are designed to help you be conscious of how much of a mess you're making by pointing out ways to overcome the common pitfalls. Whether you're outside at a campfire or in a small kitchen, cooking is always more enjoyable (and tastier, too) if your cooking space is clean, organized, and stores only the ingredients and tools you absolutely need.

BANANA PANCAKES

When cooking in small spaces it's important to use as few pieces of equipment as possible. For this recipe, there's no need to reach for a whisk (an inherently difficult tool to clean) when you can just use a fork and save yourself the time and effort of cleaning an extra tool. These banana pancakes are particularly rich and filling. The starches of the banana allow you to use less flour. And the richness of the peanut butter keeps them moist and creamy.

2 bananas, divided

1 tbsp creamy peanut butter

1 tsp granulated sugar

1 egg

½ cup (60g) self-rising flour, such as Bisquick

2 tbsp butter, plus more to serve

Maple syrup, to serve

1 Begin by preparing your heat source. You'll need a fire or a stovetop burner set at medium-high heat.

2 In a medium bowl, use a fork to mash together 1 banana and the peanut butter.

3 Add the sugar, egg, and ¼ cup (60ml) of water to the bowl and whisk with a fork until combined. Add the flour and mix until just combined.

4 Heat a large cast-iron skillet or flat top to medium-high heat. Thinly slice the remaining banana into rounds.

5 Melt the butter in the hot skillet. To form each pancake, place 3 slices of banana on the skillet and gently pour a spoonful of batter over top of the sliced banana.

6 Cook for 3 minutes or until bubbles begin to form on the surface of the batter and a spatula easily slides under the pancake. Flip and cook for 1 minute more.

7 Serve the pancakes topped with butter and maple syrup.

One way to be prepared for a quick-and-easy breakfast like this is to have premade baking mix on hand. I'm not ashamed to say I keep Bisquick around to make my streusel, cobblers, pies, and cookies. For virtually anything you want to bake, you can use Bisquick and eliminate the need to carry multiple ingredients.

BRUSSELS SPROUTS & BACON

When cooking in a small space, it's important to make the most out of using just one pan. By searing the bacon first, adding the onions next to deglaze, followed by the Brussels sprouts to soak up all the flavor and caramelize, we're building up layers of flavor in one pan. This recipe is great to cook when you only have access to one or two burners. You'll get the most flavor with the smallest amount of footprint or cleanup.

½lb (225g) bacon, diced

15–20 Brussels sprouts, bottoms removed, shaved or shredded

½ white or yellow onion, thinly sliced

2 garlic cloves, diced

2 tbsp olive oil

½ cup (50g) shaved Parmesan cheese

Zest of 1 lemon

Balsamic vinaigrette, to serve

Salt and pepper, to taste

1 Begin by preparing your heat source. You'll need a fire or a stovetop burner set at medium-high heat.

2 Add the bacon and cook until the fat is completely rendered, about 10 minutes, or until the bacon is crispy and golden brown. Drain the fat.

3 Add the Brussels sprouts, onion, garlic, and olive oil. Don't stir; instead, press down to ensure that the Brussels sprouts completely caramelize.

4 You can check for caramelization by flipping a sprout or two to ensure that the side touching the pan is a dark golden brown. This can take up to 10 minutes.

5 Once the sprouts are caramelized, remove from the heat and top with the Parmesan cheese, lemon zest, and balsamic vinaigrette. Sprinkle with salt and pepper to taste.

When I make this dish, I like to shave the Brussels sprouts. It's important you don't cut them too thin but also don't just cut them in half. All the little shaved bits will crisp up and add a nice flavor and texture to this dish.

HUSH PUPS

These tender nuggets of fried cornmeal studded with pepper and onion make a perfect companion to a spicy stew, or simply served as an appetizer with ketchup for dipping. In a small space, it can be challenging to stay clean and organized—especially when deep frying—but these hushpuppies are surprisingly easy. Don't be intimidated; all you really need is one bowl and one cast-iron pan or Dutch oven.

2 tbsp butter, melted, divided

½ green bell pepper, finely diced

1 jalapeño, finely diced (with seeds if you like things spicy)

½ white onion, finely diced

1 egg

1 (15oz/425g) can cream-style sweet corn

1 cup (120g) all-purpose flour

1 cup (160g) yellow cornmeal

2 tbsp baking powder

2 tbsp granulated sugar

1 tsp salt

1qt (1L) cooking oil, for frying

1 Begin by preparing your heat source. You'll need a fire, a grill, or a stovetop burner set at medium-high heat.

2 To a large skillet, add 1 tablespoon of the butter and sauté the bell pepper, jalapeño, and onion for 5 minutes or until translucent. Set aside to cool.

3 In a large bowl, mix together the egg, 1 tablespoon butter, corn, flour, cornmeal, baking powder, sugar, and salt until well combined. Stir in the sautéed onion and peppers, mixing until just incorporated.

4 In a large Dutch oven or deep cast-iron skillet, heat the cooking oil over medium-high heat to 350°F (180°C). To test the temperature, drop a little bit of batter into the oil; if it bubbles immediately and floats, you're ready to go.

5 Working in batches, carefully add scoops of batter to the hot oil, taking care not to crowd the pan. Cook for 3 to 4 minutes until the bottoms are golden brown, then flip and cook on the opposite side for 3 to 4 minutes more. Pull one out and crack it open to make sure it's fully cooked through and fluffy on the inside.

6 When cooked, remove the hushpuppies from the oil and place on paper towels or a cooling rack to drain; season with salt immediately. I like to eat these with ketchup.

This recipe is a great example of when not to overcrowd a pan. Rarely is it a good idea to put too much ingredient in a vessel while trying to cook it evenly. If you overcrowd this pan, the oil temp will drop well below 350°F.

ROMAINE CAESAR SALAD
WITH HOMEMADE DRESSING

Caesar dressing only has a few ingredients. It's super easy to make and creates a world of a difference for your Caesar salad when you have fresh homemade dressing. If you bring the staple ingredients for Caesar dressing with you on the go, you'll also have the components for all sorts of other dishes. A grilled romaine Caesar salad is an excellent alternative for this salad if you want to take this recipe to the next level. Simply slice the romaine heart in half, lightly oil, and don't season until off the grill.

FOR THE DRESSING:

- 1 (2oz/55g) tin anchovies
- 2 garlic cloves, minced and mashed to a paste
- 1 cup (100g) grated Parmesan cheese
- 1 egg yolk
- 2 tbsp Dijon mustard
- Juice of 1 lemon
- ½ cup (120ml) olive oil
- 2 tbsp Worcestershire sauce
- Salt and pepper, to taste

FOR THE SALAD:

- 2 slices sourdough bread, cubed
- 1 tbsp olive oil
- 1 tsp salt
- 1 tsp pepper
- 1 head romaine lettuce, washed and chopped
- 1 cup (100g) shredded Parmesan cheese
- 1 lemon, cut into wedges, to serve

FOR THE DRESSING:

1 To a medium-sized bowl, add the anchovies. Mash thoroughly with a fork. Two forks working together is a great technique to use here.

2 Add the garlic to the anchovies and mix to combine.

3 Add the Parmesan cheese to the bowl. Mix.

4 Whisk in 1 egg yolk.

5 Add the mustard, lemon juice, olive oil, and Worcestershire sauce to the bowl. Whisk to thoroughly combine. Season with salt and pepper to taste.

FOR THE SALAD:

6 Begin by preparing your heat source. You'll need a fire or a stovetop burner set at medium-low heat.

7 In a large skillet, toast the sourdough cubes with the olive oil, salt, and pepper until crunchy and crouton-like. This should take about 15 minutes. Set the croutons aside.

8 Add the romaine to one large bowl or smaller bowls depending on how you want to serve the salad. Dress the salad using the homemade Caesar dressing. Toss in the bowl(s) to thoroughly cover the romaine with the dressing.

9 Garnish with the croutons and Parmesan cheese, and serve with the lemon wedges.

If you double or triple the recipe ingredients, you'll have leftover dressing you can jar up and store to use for future salads.

VEGETABLE SOUP

There's nothing cozier in the winter than my little cabin with a roaring fire and this soup simmering away on the stovetop, filling my small space with its savory aroma. Cooking the vegetables in stages creates layers of flavor for a delicious and complex vegetable soup that's also quick and easy to make without creating a mess of a tiny kitchen.

3 tbsp olive oil

1 yellow onion, diced

3 ribs celery, diced

1 large carrot, diced

3 garlic cloves, minced

½ yellow squash, diced

½ zucchini, diced

2qt (2L) high-quality vegetable broth

1 large Russet potato, peeled and diced

1 tomato, diced

A few sprigs thyme

1 tbsp apple cider vinegar

Salt and pepper, to taste

Fresh herbs (optional), to garnish

1 Begin by preparing your heat source. You'll need a fire or a stovetop burner set at medium-high heat.

2 In a large pot, heat the olive oil over medium-high heat. Add the onion, celery, carrot, and garlic. Cook for 5 to 7 minutes, stirring occasionally, until the onion is translucent and the vegetables have begun to caramelize.

3 Push the veggies to one side of the pot, and add the yellow squash and zucchini to the clear space. Cook without stirring for about 5 minutes, allowing the squash and zucchini to caramelize.

4 Add the vegetable broth, potato, tomato, and thyme. Bring to a simmer and add the vinegar, salt, and pepper. Simmer for 30 minutes, or until the potatoes are tender.

5 Remove the thyme stems and taste to adjust the seasoning as needed before serving. Garnish with chopped fresh herbs, if desired.

This soup also freezes very well. I like to put soups like this into zip-top bags and freeze them flat, which allows for easy storage and travel.

T-BONE STEAKS
WITH CHIMICHURRI

If you're looking for a way to make your steaks explode with flavor—without grilling, using a sous vide method, or marinating them for hours and hours—make a chimichurri! The depth and complexity of the flavors in chimichurri makes it the perfect complement to a variety of dishes, not just steaks. You can make this in advance of cooking the meat. When the meat is done, let it rest, then slice and pair it with this special condiment. Tangy, spicy, salty, herbaceous, and aromatic—chimichurri packs a huge punch.

1 bunch flat-leaf parsley, finely diced

3 garlic cloves, minced

½ red onion, finely diced

½ cup (120ml) red wine vinegar

¾ cup (180ml) olive oil

1 tbsp red chili flakes

Salt and pepper, to taste

2lb (1kg) T-bone steaks

1 Begin by preparing your heat source. You'll need a fire or a grill preheated to 400°F (200°C).

2 To a large bowl, add the parsley, garlic, and onion. Mix.

3 Add the vinegar, olive oil, chili flakes, and salt and pepper.

4 Mix all the chimichurri ingredients together and adjust with more salt as needed.

5 Liberally coat the steaks with salt and pepper.

6 Sear on one side for 5 minutes. Flip the steaks and continue cooking on the other side for an additional 5 minutes or until the internal temperature has reached 125°F (50°C).

7 Let the steaks rest for 10 minutes before slicing. Drizzle on the chimichurri and enjoy!

This is great for entertaining and stores well overnight. Serve it immediately for the brightest green color or serve later for the best flavor.

IN A SMALL SPACE 201

LAMB SHANKS
WITH TOMATO-APPLE GRAVY

About ten years ago, I was cooking for a predominantly South African crew on a boat. These folks were constantly requesting dishes from their homeland that I had never tasted, let alone cooked. While we were away at sea, the homesick crew desired foods that reminded them of their lives. One of these was this dish, which uses a tomato-apple gravy. In my mind, tomato and gravy don't really go together since tomatoes themselves are thickeners. My first try at making this dish was a disaster and the entire crew disapproved of my attempt. It wasn't until the third try that I captured the flavors they'd all desired. As the sole chef on a yacht, I usually had no mentor or guide whom I could ask questions, so I learned a lot from the various crew members I worked with. Making this dish and perfecting it was satisfying not only for my crew, as they were able to enjoy something they'd been missing for so long, but also for me as a chef, receiving guidance and education. You can make this dish easily even if room is limited, and with the stew cooking for a few hours, it'll make your small space smell incredible.

2 lamb shanks

3 tbsp olive oil, divided

2 tbsp salt, divided

1½ tbsp pepper, divided

1 small white onion, diced

3 garlic cloves, diced

1 jalapeño, diced

1 Honeycrisp apple, diced

2 Roma tomatoes, diced

1 bay leaf

4 cups (960ml) beef broth

2 tbsp coriander seeds, toasted and crushed

1 tbsp cornstarch

2 sprigs rosemary

1 cup (190g) basmati rice

1 Begin by preparing your heat source. You'll need a fire or a stovetop burner set at medium-high heat.

2 Pat the lamb shanks dry. Season with 2 tablespoons olive oil, 1 tablespoon salt, and 1 tablespoon pepper.

3 Add the remaining olive oil to a Dutch oven or cast-iron pot with a lid. Bring the pot to medium-high heat.

4 Place the lamb shanks in the pot and sear on all sides until dark brown and heavily caramelized.

5 Remove the shanks and set aside temporarily.

6 To the pot, add the onion, garlic, jalapeño, and apple. Sauté for 5 to 10 minutes, until translucent.

7 Reintroduce the lamb shanks along with the tomatoes, bay leaf, beef broth, coriander seeds, 1 tablespoon salt, and ½ tablespoon pepper. Place the lid on top and reduce the heat to low.

8 Simmer for up to 4 hours. The meat should be fall-off-the-bone tender. If it is not after 4 hours, continue cooking until it is.

9 Once tender, shred the meat off the bone directly in the pot using a fork.

10 To a small bowl, add the cornstarch and 4 tablespoons water. Mix well to form a slurry. Add the mixture to the stew and bring to a boil to test the thickness. Reduce the heat to low.

11   Add the rosemary to the pot.

12   Cook the rice according to the package instructions. Fluff with a fork once cooked. Remove the bay leaf.

13   Serve the lamb with the gravy over top of the steamed rice and enjoy!

Working with cornstarch can be incredibly useful. Making a cornstarch slurry is a fast and effective way to thicken liquids. This stew without a slurry or roux would be too brothy, so we add the cornstarch slurry in at the end to adjust its thickness. If the viscosity of your dish is too thin, try adding more cornstarch. If it's too thick, add a bit of broth until you reach your desired consistency. You won't know how thick it's going to be until it's been brought to a boil.

BRIGADEIROS

Brigadeiros are the perfect sweet treat to make in a small space. With this recipe, you can create a delicious dessert using only a few ingredients and tools. The simplicity of the ingredients and the use of only one pot makes cleanup simple, and the small footprint of space needed to prepare this recipe means it can be made anywhere. This is also a great dessert for entertaining. You can build a brigadeiro bar with any of your favorite toppings, such as crushed nuts, coconut shavings, crushed chocolate bars, sprinkles, or powdered sugar.

1 tbsp butter

14oz (397g) can sweetened condensed milk

¼ cup (30g) cocoa powder

FOR THE TOPPINGS:

Sugar streusel

Crushed nuts

Crushed chocolate bars

Sprinkles

Coconut shavings

Powdered sugar

1 Begin by preparing your heat source. You'll need a fire or a stovetop burner set at low heat.

2 To a medium sauce pot, add the butter and sweetened condensed milk. Slowly add the cocoa powder, stirring each time until it fully dissolves before adding more. Continue warming until the butter is melted, and stir until smooth. This should take 15 to 20 minutes.

3 Remove the mixture from the heat. Let cool to room temperature. Place the pot directly in a refrigerator or cooler if you have one, allowing the mixture to cool for 20 to 30 minutes more.

4 In a medium bowl, mix together your desired toppings.

5 Remove the mixture from the refrigerator and roll 1 tablespoon of the mixture with two hands until it forms a small, smooth ball. Roll the ball in your toppings until evenly coated.

6 Repeat this step until all the brigadeiros are coated. Serve with fresh fruit and enjoy!

For a firmer brigadeiro, add an additional tablespoon of cocoa powder to your mixture.

CROSS-UTILIZATION

Cross-utilization is the basis of all smart and practical cookery. It is the idea of bringing as few ingredients as possible, and making as many dishes as possible from those few ingredients. Often, when you analyze a menu from a restaurant, you'll notice the same ingredient being used multiple times. This is an example of a chef cross-utilizing their ingredients to produce as many different recipe combinations as they can. This minimizes the need for a plethora of ingredients and allows the chef to focus on ordering only a few staples, which will create many different dishes while also saving money. Of course, it's important to consider cross-utilization when purchasing your ingredients, but it's equally important to use this technique when it comes to your leftovers.

Generally, when cooking, there are ingredients left over, including celery, onions, carrots, herbs, and even proteins. These are just a few of the thousands of different ingredients you might be able to use to make something new. By cross-utilizing these ingredients, you can create more delicious dishes. I genuinely believe that cross-utilization is an integral part of cooking, and the end goal for every chef should always be to use every piece of every available ingredient.

At some point, you may find yourself standing in front of a random assortment of leftover ingredients and thinking, *What can I do with this?* Before you know it, you'll be thinking of how to use the ingredients available to make a new recipe. As good cooks, we need to be flexible with our ingredients, always willing to bend the rules and try new things. Don't feel bound to a recipe or technique just because it's been written down. Be willing to make adjustments, and I bet you'll find yourself being more successful in the kitchen.

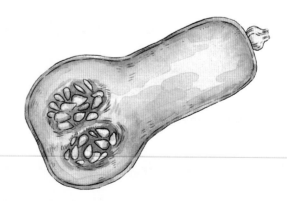

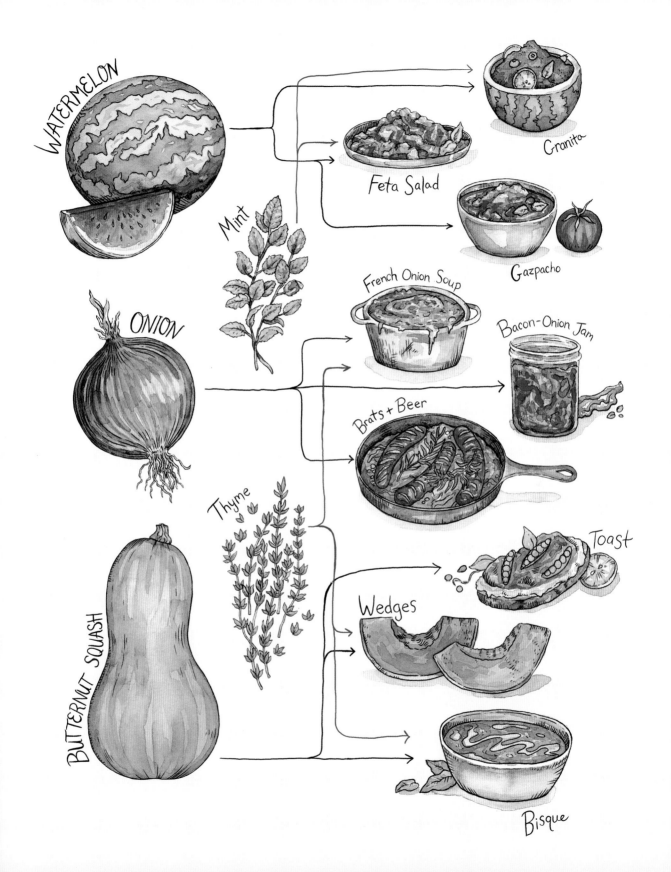

WATERMELON

Mint

ONION

Thyme

BUTTERNUT SQUASH

Feta Salad

Granita

Gazpacho

French Onion Soup

Bacon-Onion Jam

Brats + Beer

Toast

Wedges

Bisque

There are thousands of different ingredients that can be cross-utilized in countless ways. The sky really is the limit, and new recipe combinations are thought up by chefs and home cooks every day. In this chapter, I cross-utilize three different ingredients, leading to nine separate, distinct recipes. By using the foundational ingredients of watermelon, onion, and butternut squash in various ways, my goal is to show you that you're not limited to just one recipe that you may or may not have initially purchased that ingredient for. In fact, one ingredient can often provide a variety of distinct flavors and textures when used differently as the base of a new dish.

For example, it's rare that we need to use or consume an entire watermelon for just one recipe. Many times, half of it gets put away to be sliced up later, or is forgotten about altogether. But what if you could use that other half to make Watermelon Gazpacho, or Watermelon & Feta Salad? Or better yet, what if you used each half of the watermelon to create both recipes simultaneously from the outset? This is the very definition of cross-utilization.

Another, perhaps more obvious example is the beloved onion. Regardless of whether you love or hate onions, it's important to understand they're the base of most savory dishes worldwide. This powerhouse ingredient adds robust flavor and can be transformed into an infinite number of dishes. It can be the star of the show like in French Onion Soup, or used to create a side dish or topping, like Bacon-Onion Jam. By keeping onions on hand, you're effectively exercising what it means to cross-utilize. Stocking onions and other easily adaptable ingredients in your home kitchen or packing them when you're cooking on the go will show you the benefits of creating recipes that fully utilize every component.

WATERMELON MINT GRANITA

Most options available for off-road refrigeration don't come with a powerful freezer. They can freeze things, sure, but it usually takes a long time and the vehicle must be still. Watermelon mint granita is a dessert that can still reach the perfect level of chilled using these less-than-ideal freezers. A granita is basically a flavorful slush, and it's incredibly refreshing in hot environments. Clean, vibrant, and airy, this recipe will leave your sweet tooth satisfied.

1 small watermelon (any fruit will work if watermelon isn't in season), about 5lb (2.3kg)

½ cup (100g) granulated sugar

2 tsp salt

1 bunch mint, minced, plus more to garnish

1 Begin by mashing up your fruit. Use a blender or immersion blender if available. Otherwise, you can pulverize your watermelon by dicing it first, and then adding it to a zip-top bag and mashing the fruit by hand.

2 Add the sugar, salt, and herbs. Blend or mix thoroughly until all ingredients are dissolved and the mixture has reached a smooth consistency without lumps.

3 Pour the mixture into a freezer-safe dish or zip-top bag. Let it sit in the freezer for 30-minute increments, removing from the freezer each time to stir, scraping down the edges before returning to the freezer. Repeat this process until a slushy texture forms. This could take up to 2 hours.

If you have an immersion blender, you can use it to easily create this refreshing treat.

WATERMELON & FETA SALAD
WITH BALSAMIC GLAZE

When cooking in confined spaces, you want to make low-maintenance dishes with easy cleanup. You only need to dirty a cutting board and one knife to make this simple yet impressive salad, and it's incredibly satisfying on a hot summer day. Serve it as a side dish (you could even serve it as a platter on the cutting board), and use the other half of the watermelon to make granita for dessert—100 percent utilization.

6 cups (912g) watermelon, cut into cubes (from about one half of a small seedless watermelon)

½ red onion, thinly sliced

1 English cucumber, sliced rondelle

1 cup (160g) crumbled feta

¼ cup (60ml) olive oil

2–3 tbsp balsamic glaze

Salt and pepper, to taste

1 On a platter or in a wide, shallow bowl, layer the watermelon, onion, cucumber, and feta.

2 Drizzle olive oil and balsamic glaze over the top, and season with salt and pepper.

Remove the top and bottom of the watermelon, allowing it to stand upright easily. Work your knife from top to bottom in a sawing motion, following the curve of the watermelon to the bottom. Repeat this action all the way around the melon. Or, only skin half and preserve the rest of it for later.

WATERMELON GAZPACHO

All the ingredients in this gazpacho are easily cross-utilized and can be used in other dishes before or after making this recipe. For example, if you use half a watermelon at lunch to prepare a salad with cucumber and feta, the leftover ingredients can be used to make this quick-and-easy gazpacho later in the day or the following day. That way, you'll utilize all your ingredients, with nothing going to waste. Gazpacho is a dish most people don't fully understand, but once you try it, this recipe will become a staple among your summer favorites. It's light and refreshing on a hot afternoon.

½ watermelon, rind removed, cubed (1 cup [152g] reserved)

2 Roma tomatoes, roughly chopped

1 jalapeño, roughly chopped

1 red onion (½ roughly chopped, ½ diced)

1 cucumber, peeled (½ roughly chopped, ½ diced)

½ cup mint, minced (reserve 3–4 leaves for garnish)

1 tbsp olive oil

2 tbsp red wine vinegar

Pinch of salt and pepper

½ cup (80g) feta, crumbled

Basil leaves, to garnish

1 Fill a blender with the watermelon cubes, reserving a cup of the cubes to use later as toppings. Purée the fruit until smooth.

2 Add the tomatoes, jalapeño, half the onion (chopped), half the cucumber (chopped), and mint to the blender along with the olive oil, the red wine vinegar, and the salt and pepper.

3 Blend thoroughly until well combined and no lumps remain. Taste, and add more salt and pepper to your liking. Refrigerate the mixture.

4 While the gazpacho is cooling, prepare your toppings in a medium bowl by combining the remaining watermelon cubes, red onion, and cucumber. Toss to make a salad.

5 Once the gazpacho is thoroughly cooled (at least 1 hour), pour it into bowls and top with the salad, feta, and basil.

This can be made and stored frozen in advance. Once you get to your campsite, simply thaw it out and prepare your toppings.

BACON-ONION JAM

Anyone and everyone can make a burger or sandwich, but how do we elevate it? Condiments are the answer. This bacon jam is an excellent way to add a huge punch of flavor to an otherwise ordinary dish; simply slather it onto your bun and prepare for a majorly better burger.

1lb (450g) thick-cut bacon, chopped into ½-inch (1.25cm) pieces

1 large sweet onion, diced

¼ cup (60ml) red wine vinegar

¼ cup (50g) sugar

1 tsp salt

1–2 sprigs thyme, leaves only

1 Begin by preparing your heat source. You'll need a fire or a stovetop burner set at medium-low heat.

2 In a large saucepan over medium-low heat, cook the bacon for 8 to 10 minutes, until the fat has rendered and the bacon is crisp. Transfer the cooked bacon to a plate lined with paper towels and set aside. Drain the rendered fat from the pan, leaving about 1 tablespoon behind.

3 To the same pan, add the onion and cook over medium heat for 5 minutes or until translucent. Reduce the heat to low and continue to caramelize for 15 minutes or until golden brown.

4 Add the bacon, vinegar, sugar, salt, and ¼ cup (60ml) water. Simmer for 20 minutes or until the jam has thickened.

5 Remove from the heat and stir in the thyme. Let cool and use immediately on a burger or turkey sandwich, or transfer to jars and refrigerate until ready to use.

This jam stores well and can be made long in advance, just be sure to let it come to room temperature prior to serving.

FRENCH ONION SOUP

Given the minimal effort and attention this recipe needs, the ingredients used here pack a huge punch. Rich, savory, creamy, crunchy, brothy, aromatic, hot, and intense all at once, this soup is a world-renowned favorite for a reason. It hits all your gastronomic senses at once. Because of the high level of caramelization that occurs prior to adding the broth, this recipe transforms an ordinary vegetable (the onion) into a savory, sensory overload. This is one of my mother's favorite dishes, and it's clear why.

3 white onions, thinly sliced

1 leek, roots and green parts removed, whites thinly sliced

3 garlic cloves

¾lb (340g) butter, divided

1½ tbsp flour

½ cup (120ml) sherry wine

1qt (1L) beef broth

Salt and pepper, to taste

1 sprig thyme

1 baguette, sliced

2 cups (200g) grated Gruyère cheese

1 Begin by preparing your heat source. You'll need a fire or a stovetop burner set at medium-high heat.

2 To a large soup pot, add the onions, leek, garlic, and ½lb (225g) of the butter. Cook for about 30 minutes, or until the ingredients are golden brown. Stir occasionally, about every 5 minutes, until the moisture is cooked out of the onions. Reduce the heat to low.

3 Sprinkle the flour over the vegetables to help them soak up the butter. Mix in well.

4 Deglaze the pot by adding the sherry wine and beef broth. Mix thoroughly and bring to a low boil. Add ¼ cup (60ml) water at a time if the soup is too thick. Season with salt and pepper to taste. Add the thyme. Let simmer for 20 minutes or longer. The soup should lightly coat the back of a spoon when it's ready.

5 Spread the remaining butter onto the baguette slices and toast, using medium heat on both sides to make crostinis. You'll need one or two for each bowl you plan to serve.

6 Ladle soup into each of your bowls, place a crostini or two on top of the soup, and add the Gruyère cheese on top of the crostini.

7 Broil the assembled soup bowls on high heat until the cheese is fully melted and bubbling with a nice golden color. Be sure not to burn it! Garnish with some of the remaining thyme and enjoy!

This recipe is even better if you can prepare your own delicious beef broth. If you don't have time to do so, purchase the best possible beef broth you can find. The darker the stock the better.

BRATS & BEER

If you're looking to impress at your next cookout, these beer brats with caramelized onions are sure to be a hit. The onions help to elevate that boring brat-and-ketchup game to the next level. This recipe is a fast and simple way to bring life to an otherwise timeless dish.

4 high-quality bratwursts, both sides scored

1 tbsp butter or olive oil

1 white onion, thinly sliced

2 garlic cloves, sliced

1 tbsp mustard, plus extra to garnish

1 tbsp flour

Pinch of salt and pepper

1 (12oz/340g) can stout or other dark beer

4 sliced buns

Rosemary sprigs, to garnish

1 Begin by preparing your heat source. You'll need a fire, a grill, or a stovetop burner set at medium-high heat.

2 Over your heat source, give the bratwursts a quick char on both sides, then set aside.

3 Grease a large cast-iron pan with the butter or olive oil.

4 Add the onion to the greased pan and cook down for 20 minutes, or until golden brown in color.

5 Add the garlic, mustard, flour, and salt and pepper. Stir until mixed thoroughly.

6 Deglaze the pan with the beer, slowly pouring the entire can over the cooking ingredients while stirring until the beer resembles a sauce.

7 Add the bratwursts back to the pan.

8 Let simmer for an additional 10 minutes.

9 Place the bratwursts in the buns with the extra mustard and a scoop of the onions. Garnish with the rosemary. Enjoy the delicious broth by dipping your finished brats in it as you take one tasty bite after another!

I like using dark beer for this recipe, like a stout. I don't recommend an IPA, as it will turn out tasting too bitter.

BUTTERNUT WEDGES
WITH SAGE PESTO

Sage is an underutilized herb, but it shines in this recipe. Sweet butternut squash wedges are tossed with a fresh sage and pecan pesto for a flavor and texture combination that appeals to all the senses. I like to make this dish in a cast-iron pan on the grill, which makes an excellent alternative oven. When the grill thermometer reaches 375° to 400°F (190° to 200°C) on the grill thermometer, you're ready to bake, just like your kitchen oven. And you can use the remaining half of the butternut squash to make Butternut Squash Bisque (page 229).

2 bunches sage, leaves only (reserve a few leaves for garnish)

1 cup (125g) chopped pecans

1 cup (100g) Parmesan cheese, half grated, half shredded

Zest and juice of 2 lemons

4 tbsp olive oil, plus extra to garnish

Salt and pepper, to taste

½ butternut squash, peeled and cut into 1-inch (2.5cm) wide wedges

1 Begin by preparing your heat source. You'll need a grill or an oven preheated to 400°F (200°C).

2 To make the pesto, in a food processor, combine the sage leaves, pecans, and ½ cup (50g) of the Parmesan cheese. Pulse to combine. With the food processor on, slowly add the lemon zest, lemon juice, and olive oil. Blend until a slightly chunky pesto forms. Taste and season with salt and pepper as needed. Pulse once more to combine.

3 In a large bowl, combine the pesto and squash and toss until the squash is well coated. Arrange the squash in a single layer in a cast-ion skillet or on a baking sheet.

4 Place on your grill (lid closed) or in the oven and roast for about 30 minutes or until the squash is fork-tender.

5 Shred the remaining ½ cup (50g) Parmesan cheese over the roasted squash. (I use a peeler.) Top with a few fresh sage leaves and a drizzle of olive oil.

This dish is really all about the heat and the time. Not everyone's knife skills are the same, and some wedges are going to take more or less time to cook. Keep an eye on your food; if the wedges don't look delicious yet, they're probably not. Be patient and let the squash fully caramelize before removing it from the heat.

BUTTERNUT SQUASH BISQUE

Making a great bisque involves a bit of patience and cooking know-how. When making a bisque of any flavor, it's most important to extract as much flavor from the ingredients as possible before adding your liquids. In the case of this bisque we heavily roast our butternut squash and vegetables for 45 minutes. This ensures that each vegetable has caramelized and concentrated its flavors. We then combine all the ingredients to form a delicious well-rounded soup. You can even substitute the squash with a variety of other bases, like lobster, mushrooms, or celery. The range of bisques is infinite and deserves some exploration.

½ butternut squash, unpeeled, seeds removed

4 tbsp olive oil, divided

1 white onion, peeled and halved

3 ribs celery, roughly chopped

¼ large carrot

1 tomato, halved

1 head garlic, halved horizontally

2qt (2L) chicken stock

A few sprigs thyme

1 tbsp apple cider vinegar

Salt and pepper, to taste

¼ cup (60g) sour cream, to serve

Chopped chives, to garnish

1 Begin by preparing your heat source. You'll need a fire, a grill, or an oven preheated to 400°F (200°C).

2 Score the skin of the squash a few times, cutting about ½ inch (1.5cm) deep. Coat the squash with 1 tablespoon of the olive oil and place it cut side down on a large cast-iron pan or baking sheet.

3 Coat the onion, celery, carrot, tomato, and garlic with the remaining 3 tablespoons olive oil and arrange on the pan around the squash.

4 Place on the grill (lid closed) or in the oven and roast for about 45 minutes, or until the butternut squash is fork-tender. Remove from the grill or oven and let cool.

5 Scoop the flesh of the roasted squash into a large soup pot (discard the skin). Add the other roasted vegetables to the pot, squeezing the roasted garlic from its skin. Add the chicken stock, thyme, and apple cider vinegar.

6 Place on the stovetop over medium-high heat and bring to a boil. When boiling, reduce the heat to a simmer and cook for 20 minutes.

7 Remove the thyme sprigs from the soup. Using a blender or immersion blender, blend the soup until it's completely smooth. Taste and season with salt and pepper.

8 Serve topped with a dollop of sour cream and garnish with the chives.

An immersion blender is by far the easiest was to make this; however, it will be slightly more textured than your typical bisque. If you have a blender handy, let it run twice as long as you'd think; this ensures a particularly creamy and smooth soup. You could take another step and strain out any additional large matter prior to serving.

CROSS-UTILIZATION 229

BUTTERNUT TOAST
WITH RICOTTA & PEAS

When I'm choosing ingredients at the store to cross-utilize, I like to pick items that last a long time. Foods like squash, onions, apples, oranges, corn, potatoes, and carrots always work well. For this recipe, we use butternut squash, which is an incredibly durable vegetable. It can last for weeks at room temperature, and can be transformed into a variety of different dishes. One of my favorite things to make with butternut squash is this toast, which is unlike anything you've ever eaten. The savory taste of the grilled squash, the crunch and sweet pop of the ripe English pea, and the tangy smooth texture of the bright ricotta cheese all together makes this a recipe that will melt in your mouth. Balanced dishes like this one make you come back for more and more.

1 butternut squash, halved and seeds removed

4 tbsp olive oil, divided, plus extra to garnish

1 tbsp salt, divided, plus a pinch to garnish

1½ cups (375g) ricotta cheese

½ tbsp pepper, plus a pinch to garnish

Zest and juice of 1 lemon

1 loaf artisan bread, sliced

15–20 sugar snap peas

2–3 tbsp honey

1 Begin by preparing your heat source. You'll need a fire, a grill, or an oven preheated to 400°F (200°C).

2 Coat the butternut squash halves with 2 tablespoons of the olive oil and ½ tablespoon of the salt. Grill face down, until light golden brown, at least 15 minutes per side, or until the squash softens. Remove the squash from your heat source and let it cool for at least 20 minutes.

3 In a large bowl, combine the ricotta cheese, the pepper, the other ½ tablespoon of salt, and the lemon zest. Mix thoroughly.

4 Griddle thick slices of the bread in the olive oil until it becomes golden brown on both sides, while still soft in the center. This should take about 3 minutes per side.

5 Remove the toast and place it on a plate to assemble. Spread a big spoonful of the ricotta cheese mixture across the surface of the toast.

6 Using a spoon, scoop out chunks of the butternut squash and place on top of the ricotta cheese mixture.

7 Top with the sugar snap peas.

8 Finish by drizzling on the honey and the olive oil. Squeeze on some lemon juice, and add salt and pepper to taste.

> By picking foods that last a long time at room temperature, you can ensure ample time to create multiple recipes before your ingredients expire.

LESS IS MORE

Each year that I cook professionally it seems I strip away more and more ingredients from my grocery list. I used to be notorious for having every food item under the sun, just in case I needed to use it in a backup plan. To be honest with you, I mistakenly believed that having a lot of ingredients meant whatever I made with them would taste good. I couldn't have been more wrong.

As I'm getting older and settling more into what I find to be my ideal cooking style, I've realized that limiting the number of different ingredients I use has been a big part of that. When people see me cook, they often comment on how few ingredients I'm using. "How did you get that to taste so good?" is a question I hear all the time. My answer is usually something along the lines of, "A few very high-quality ingredients will trump a bunch of nonsense any day." As time has gone on, my recipes have gotten more and more simple.

The mindset to simplify has come about because of different factors. My experiences cooking for high-net-worth individuals led me to believe I had to have the best ingredients, and a lot of them. This mentality was ingrained in me early in my culinary career, and resulted in cooking tons of complicated recipes with dozens of ingredients. Eventually, I realized I was creating way more work for myself. To overcome this, I learned ways to responsibly cut corners, which saved me both time and money. In doing so, the light of possibilities shone through, and new recipes were born. I was able to be more creative, and I didn't feel tied down by the constraints of the recipes I was following.

When you let go of what you've learned, become willing to experiment with new things, and consider all the ways to cook more with less, this is when the chef inside is born.

Good Coffee

Blackberries

fig 1. Rubus allegheniensis

"Less is more" is a style of cooking that will improve your skills; make you think independently; save you time, money, and effort; and teach you how to source the most essential high-quality ingredients. I believe that following this mindset will also teach you how to appreciate the flavors that each individual ingredient provides, which expands your palate. Cooking with less is also ideal for the traveler or nomad. This vagabond style of cooking on the road teaches you how to work with what you have and make the most of very little. The challenge of using limited ingredients has led me to create some of the simplest and most delicious meals I've ever made.

When you're using less to make something, each ingredient becomes all the more important, allowing you to focus on creating the perfect flavor combinations. Instead of adding in a bunch of different ingredients that might blend together and mask each other's flavors, each individual ingredient adds to the finished dish in a critical way that will be apparent on your palate when you take that first bite. This approach also helps you to be prepared more easily, as you only need to pack up a few items to make these focused, simpler recipes while you're on the go.

The recipes in this chapter are only a few examples of what it means to consider less being more. I encourage you to incorporate this way of cooking into your life, how you travel, and how you see the world. Complicating and overcrowding recipes rarely makes them better. Many great restaurants feature a concise, focused menu that has just a few amazing choices, and nothing is mediocre. You can apply this same kind of mentality to the kinds of recipes you make and pair together, only focusing on the very best. The less you use, the more you'll get in return.

ANY BERRY JAM

If you're picking berries yourself, it's important to make sure your berries are ripe if you're planning to make jam with them, because if they are harvested too early, the flavor will be much tarter than it should be. The lesson here is that whenever you're making something with only a few key ingredients, you must make sure those two or three ingredients are top-notch quality. In the case of this jam, I pick the ripe berries myself, which guarantees a delicious jam. If you can't pick berries yourself, store-bought berries should already be the appropriate ripeness. If you have any berries that are overripe, these can be some of the best berries to use in a jam.

2–2½lb (1kg) of any kind of berry

1 cup (200g) granulated sugar

1 tsp salt

1 lemon rind

1 Begin by preparing your heat source. You'll need a fire or a stovetop burner set at medium-low heat.

2 Wash all the berries thoroughly. Don't worry about drying them.

3 To a medium-sized sauce pot, add all the berries.

4 Add the sugar, salt, lemon rind, and 3 tablespoons water. Mix to combine.

5 Let the berry mixture simmer over medium-low heat for up to 1 hour, crushing the berries with a fork periodically. Once it starts to thicken, you will notice a syrupy consistency. At this point, the mixture should coat the back of a spoon and the bubbles in the mixture should be slower to burst.

6 To check if the jam is done cooking, remove a small spoonful and place on a plate and let it cool in the fridge for 10 minutes. This will reveal the jam's final consistency. If the jam is thick and holds its shape, it's finished. You can now remove it from the heat. While testing the thickness, keep the rest of the jam off the heat to prevent overthickening.

7 Prior to jarring, remove the lemon rind. Spoon the mixture into lidded mason jars and keep it refrigerated.

It can be so much fun to forage for berries or to buy them at your local farmers market or fruit stand. If you own land, plant some bushes to have berries for years to come! All types of berries work in this recipe. For example, a blackberry jam will have a tarter flavor than a blueberry jam, which will be sweeter. Don't limit your jam to one type of berry. You can mix berries, such as a blended berry jam with blackberry, blueberry, and raspberry.

FRENCH LOVE NUGGETS

I first made these sweet, sausage-stuffed rolls when I was cooking for a family with three little boys. All of the kids loved French toast and maple sausages, separately. One day I decided to try stuffing some sweet rolls with their favorite breakfast item, and the love nugget was born. If you're cooking for kids, this one is sure to be a winner. They're simple to make and very pleasing to eat for both kids and adults.

24 breakfast sausage links (maple flavor recommended)

24 Hawaiian sweet rolls

6 eggs

1 cup (240ml) cream or half-and-half

2 tbsp granulated sugar

1 tsp ground cinnamon

8 tbsp butter, divided

TO SERVE:

Maple syrup

Powdered sugar

Fresh berries

1 Begin by preparing your heat source. You'll need a fire, a grill, or a stovetop burner set at medium heat.

2 Cook the sausages according to package instructions until they're golden brown and juicy.

3 Using your finger or a chopstick, poke a hole horizontally through the center of each sweet roll. Insert a cooked sausage into each roll. (It's fine if the ends protrude from the sides of the roll.)

4 In a large bowl, whisk together the eggs, cream, sugar, and cinnamon.

5 Heat a griddle or large skillet over medium heat. Melt 2 tablespoons butter in the pan. Working in batches, dip the stuffed sweet rolls in the egg mixture, turning to coat. Immediately add the dipped rolls to the pan and cook, turning frequently, until golden brown on all sides. (I like to spoon a little extra egg dip onto the roll to create a "skirt" of cooked batter.)

6 Adding butter to the pan as needed, repeat the process with the remainder of the rolls.

7 Serve topped with the maple syrup, powdered sugar, and fresh berries, if desired.

When making these love nuggets, regular French toast, pancakes, or crepes, the trick is a well-seasoned, nonstick pan or cast iron with a rather excessive amount of butter. This butter is what creates the delicious golden-brown edges.

CHILAQUILES

After years of sailing around the coast of Mexico from Baja to the mainland, I've experienced dozens of versions of this Mexican breakfast. This simplified version can be adapted based on the ingredients available to you. It's a great way to utilize leftovers. If you have chicken, add it. If you have cheese, add it. If you have salsa or sour cream, go for it. Look at this recipe as the base for your chilaquiles and improvise from there.

20–30 tortilla chips

1 (10oz/283g) can red enchilada sauce

2 eggs

TO SERVE:

Sliced avocado

Fresh cilantro

Hot sauce

1 Begin by preparing your heat source. You'll need a fire or a stovetop burner set at medium heat.

2 To a large, high-sided skillet or Dutch oven, add the tortilla chips. Pour the enchilada sauce over the chips.

3 Reduce the heat to medium-low. Fold the sauce over the chips until evenly coated. Create a level surface by pressing the chips down with the back of a spoon. Don't be afraid to crush some of the chips.

4 Crack the eggs onto the surface of the chips and cover with foil or a lid. Steam for 5 to 7 minutes or until the eggs are cooked to your liking. (I like mine over easy.)

5 Serve topped with the sliced avocado, cilantro, and hot sauce.

If you don't love your eggs poached or over easy, simply scramble prior to pouring over your chips. Stir occasionally until fully cooked.

MAPLE-GLAZED CARROTS

A simple dish like this brings out the best flavors and qualities of the humble carrot, without overpowering or drawing attention away from it. I find that simple dishes are often the most crowd-pleasing. Applying a less-is-more ethos allows the flavors of a few ingredients to truly shine. I find that the simplest approach is often the tastiest.

1 tbsp butter

5–6 medium carrots, peeled and sliced lengthwise

Pinch of salt and pepper

1 tbsp brown sugar

½ cup (75g) whole roasted almonds

1 tbsp maple syrup

2 sprigs chopped rosemary, plus 1 sprig to garnish

1 Begin by preparing your heat source. You'll need a fire, a grill, or a stovetop burner set at medium heat.

2 Warm a medium-sized cast-iron skillet or other appropriate roasting pan over your heat source. Add the butter and let it melt to coat the skillet.

3 Add the carrots to the pan with the flat sides facing down.

4 Season the carrots with salt and pepper and sprinkle on the brown sugar, coating evenly.

5 Cover the skillet with a lid or tin foil and let cook for 5 minutes, allowing the carrots to steam until fork-tender.

6 Remove the lid, increase to medium-high heat, and fully caramelize the carrots, 2 to 3 minutes. Add the almonds and drizzle on the maple syrup, then remove from the heat.

7 Garnish with the rosemary, serve, and enjoy!

By limiting the number of ingredients you use in a recipe, you're forced to use good technique to let the ingredients themselves take center stage. Throwing a myriad of different ingredients all into one recipe can complicate the dish and overwhelm the flavor combinations.

PICKLED RED ONION

I didn't start enjoying pickled flavors until later in life. As time went on and my palate developed, I realized what a great accompaniment something like pickled onions can be. I like how we can transform the ordinary flavor of an onion into a flavor explosion as a condiment to your favorite and most common dishes. Try adding pickled onion to your next burger, taco, sandwich, or salad, and elevate that dish to a level you've never experienced before. Unlike sauerkraut or other fermented dishes, these pickled onions are ready to eat within an hour and only get better with time.

1 medium red onion

1 tbsp granulated sugar

2 tsp salt

2 tsp black pepper

⅓ cup (80ml) red wine vinegar

1 Cut the red onion in half lengthwise and then slice as thinly as possible into half moons. (A mandoline slicer is useful if you have one.)

2 To a 16oz mason jar with a lid, add the sugar, salt, pepper, vinegar, and ½ cup (120ml) water. Secure the lid and give it a good shake.

3 Remove the lid and stuff the jar full of the red onion—all the way to the top. Really cram it in there!

4 Let marinate for a minimum of 1 hour before using. If stored in the refrigerator, this can be enjoyed for up to 2 weeks.

The thinner you cut the onion slices, the better the final mouth appeal. These should be more shaved onions than sliced—about ⅛ inch (3mm) in width, no thicker than your fingernail. If you can't achieve this, that's okay; they will still be delicious, just a bit crunchier and with more onion flavor.

STEELHEAD WITH BLACKBERRIES

In recent years, I've found myself spending most of my time at home in the Pacific Northwest. My little cabin sits close by to world-class steelhead fishing and rivers lined with plentiful blackberries that are ripe for the taking. It didn't take long for the chef in me to realize the availability of these two ingredients made for the perfect local recipe. All I needed to bring with me was my fishing rod, a skillet, butter, some garlic, and a lemon. I recommend you fish in the morning and get yourself a fresh catch. Spend the early afternoon foraging for a hatful of fresh blackberries, and come evening, light up a fire and enjoy the accomplished feeling of making this dish from ingredients you harvested yourself.

3 tbsp butter, divided

1 steelhead trout, portioned into 2 or 3 fillets

1 tbsp salt, divided

2 tsp pepper, divided

1 shallot, diced

2 garlic cloves, minced

25–30 fresh blackberries

⅓ cup (66g) granulated sugar

1 lemon, halved

Fresh dill, to garnish (optional)

1 Begin by preparing your heat source. You'll need a fire or a stovetop burner set at medium-high heat.

2 Heat 2 tablespoons of the butter in a medium-sized cast-iron skillet on medium-high heat.

3 Season the steelhead with ½ tablespoon salt and 1 teaspoon pepper. Place the fillets flesh side down in the pan. Sear for 3 to 5 minutes or until golden brown. You want to fully caramelize this side of the trout.

4 Once fully caramelized, flip the fillet, and continue cooking for another 2 minutes, or until just fully cooked through. You'll know the fish is fully cooked when the fish is fully opaque with no transparent parts. If you're not sure, try to separate the thickest part of the fish and peek in to make sure none of it's raw. Remove the fish and transfer to a platter.

5 Add the remaining tablespoon of butter to the skillet. Let it melt. Add the shallot and garlic and cook in the butter for about 5 minutes.

6 Add the blackberries, ¼ cup water, sugar, ½ tablespoon salt, and 1 teaspoon pepper to the skillet and simmer on medium heat for 5 minutes.

7 While the blackberry sauce is simmering, grill the lemon halves on high heat so they're nice and charred.

8 At this point, the blackberries should have popped and created a beautiful sauce. If you need to help them pop, use the back of a fork to break them up and thicken your sauce.

9 Spoon the finished blackberry sauce over top of the fish filets. Garnish with fresh dill and the charred lemon halves.

> If you like a crispy skin, you can fry these skin side down without removing the skin. The skin is completely edible and delicious, though I understand it's not for everyone.

GNOCCHI
WITH DRIED MUSHROOM & CRISPY SAGE

This recipe was born of opportunity. Early in spring during my first year at my cabin, I noticed a morel mushroom growing at my doorstep. I proceeded to look for more. Lo and behold, I found dozens scattered along my driveway. It turned out my property in the woods was a treasure trove of morel mushrooms. I gathered as many as I could and decided to dry a bunch to preserve them for future use. As for the fresh mushrooms I foraged that day, I decided to make gnocchi with morels. I have a giant sage bush growing next to my house and thought: Why not add crispy sage as a garnish? The garden was already pumping out potatoes, and the eggs from my hens were plentiful. This recipe wrote itself based on the ingredients my property provided. I felt so inspired, I decided I would make gnocchi every spring when the morels popped up again. I even made my own rigagnocchi, a wooden gnocchi stripper board. Sitting by my fireplace, I hand-carved the board, knowing very well I would use it again next year.

FOR THE GNOCCHI:
2 medium baking potatoes

2 egg yolks

2 tsp salt

1 cup (120g) all-purpose flour, plus more for dusting

FOR THE SAUCE:
1½oz (40g) dried mushrooms (any variety works) or 6oz (170g) sliced fresh mushrooms

2 tbsp butter, divided in half

2 garlic cloves, minced

¼ cup (60ml) white wine

½ cup (120ml) cream

½ cup (50g) grated Parmesan cheese, plus more to garnish

Salt and pepper, to taste

Zest of 1 lemon

FOR THE SAGE GARNISH:
1 bunch sage

½ cup (120ml) olive oil

1 Begin by preparing your heat source. You'll need a fire or an oven preheated to 350°F (180°C).

2 Place the potatoes on a baking sheet and bake for 45 to 60 minutes or until fully cooked. (If you don't have access to an oven, you can peel and cube the potatoes and boil them for 25 minutes, as if you were making mashed potatoes.) Once the potatoes are fully cooked, remove from the heat and let cool.

3 When the potatoes are cool enough to handle, remove the skins. (These should peel off easily.) In a large bowl, mash the potatoes until smooth. Add the egg yolks, salt, and flour. Continue mixing until a dough is formed.

4 Turn the dough out onto a cutting board lightly dusted with flour. Roll a handful of dough into a ball. Using two hands, roll the ball into a long, thin log about ½ inch (1.25cm) thick.

5 Using a knife, cut the log of dough into 1-inch (2.5cm) sections. Coat each one with flour as it is cut. Add texture to the gnocchi by rolling each piece of dough across the back of a fork and directly onto a plate. (Once you roll the gnocchi, handle it as little as possible to avoid compromising the texture you create with the fork.) Set aside.

6 To make the crispy sage garnish, pluck each leaf from its main stem. In a small saucepan, heat the olive oil over medium-high heat, never allowing it to smoke. Test for temperature by adding 1 sage leaf. If it sizzles immediately, it's ready. Add all the sage leaves and fry for about 15 seconds or until the sizzling has ceased. Remove immediately and place on paper towels to soak up excess oil. Set aside.

7 Soak the dried mushrooms in warm water for 5 to 10 minutes or until fully rehydrated and soft. Drain and pat dry.

8 To prepare the gnocchi and sauce, heat a medium skillet over medium-high heat. Add 1 tablespoon of the butter, and make sure it is fully melted before adding the gnocchi. Cook the gnocchi for up to 5 minutes on one side until dark golden brown. Stir as little as possible.

9 Push the gnocchi to the back of the pan and add the remaining 1 tablespoon butter and rehydrated mushrooms to the cleared surface. Sauté for 2 to 3 minutes. Add the garlic and briefly sauté for 30 seconds to 1 minute. Be careful not to burn.

10 Add the wine to deglaze the pan, scraping any browned bits from the bottom. Stir in the cream, Parmesan cheese, salt, pepper, and ¼ cup (60ml) water.

11 Reduce the heat to low. Cover with a lid and simmer for up to 5 minutes, allowing the sauce to thicken and the gnocchi to cook through.

12 Stir in the lemon zest and more Parmesan cheese. Let rest for a couple of minutes, and garnish with the crispy sage and more Parmesan, if desired.

Although morels inspired this recipe, it can be prepared with countless other mushrooms, fresh or dried. Try gnocchi with chanterelles, oysters, shiitakes, or even grilled portobello.

PEACH & BLACKBERRY COBBLER

This streusel-like crumble topping has to be one of the most versatile dessert recipes available. You can make this topping and add it to just about anything fruity and it will come out perfect. I even like using it raw and unbaked as a simple garnish to add sweetness and texture. What I particularly enjoy about this recipe is the simplicity of it. Very few ingredients here, just the flavors of the fruit speaking for themselves.

1 tbsp butter

5–6 fresh semi-ripe peaches

2–3 cups (300–450g) blackberries

FOR THE TOPPING:

¾ cup (90g) all-purpose flour

1 cup (200g) granulated sugar

8 tbsp butter, melted

1 tsp salt

1 Begin by preparing your heat source. You'll need a fire, a grill, or an oven preheated to 375°F (190°C).

2 Liberally butter a large cast-iron skillet.

3 Add all of your peaches and blackberries to the skillet by alternately adding the fruit in.

4 In a bowl, mix the flour, sugar, melted butter, and salt, forming a streusel crumble.

5 Add all of the crumble to the top of the berries and peaches; don't press down, just spread it out evenly and gently.

6 Place the skillet on the grill or in the oven and bake for 45 minutes to 1 hour.

7 When the berries have burst and the crumble is golden brown, remove and let cool.

8 Enjoy with whipped cream or ice cream.

This works great with canned peaches as well, though I would add more flour to help soak up some of the moisture.

TEX'S DAILY

I don't love the idea of giving Tex dog food. As a chef, I have a special understanding of what living creatures desire to eat, and that includes our furry friends. I found Tex as a stray puppy in West Texas, and he's been with me now for six years. When I first found him, he would eat anything. He was starving. At first, I did what every dog owner does and gave him kibble. But as time went on and the great smells continued to roll from the campfire and out of my cabin kitchen, Tex eventually wouldn't eat the kibble. He would walk up to it, sniff it, and immediately walk away in disgust. I realized I had to begin making Tex his own food. I've found the best way to do that is to cook everything in one pot simultaneously. It's quick, easy, and inexpensive, and I've never seen Tex happier. At this stage, I'm not sure I'll ever give him kibble again. Please keep in mind, this recipe is just a guideline, as Tex doesn't eat this same combination every day. Be sure to research what's safe for your dog to eat before adjusting this recipe.

1 cup (190g) uncooked brown rice

2 cups (240g) frozen peas

1 sweet potato

1 rotisserie chicken

1 cup (240ml) chicken bone broth (for homemade, see page 27)

1 Begin by preparing your heat source. You'll need a fire or a stovetop burner set at low heat.

2 In a large pot, combine the rice, peas, sweet potato, and 2¼ cups (530ml) water. Cover with a lid or foil and simmer over low heat for 25 minutes.

3 Meanwhile, remove the meat from the chicken. Discard the skin and reserve the bones for bone broth. Add the shredded chicken to the pot and stir to combine.

4 Cool the mixture and serve as needed with one cup of warm chicken broth (because Tex is spoiled).

Rotisserie chicken from a local grocer is usually less expensive than a whole raw chicken, and the leftover carcass can be used to make bone broth.

ACKNOWLEDGMENTS

To my mom: you instilled within me the eye for beauty, creativity, and of course, delicious food. The worldly upbringing you provided propelled me into this life of culinary adventure and gave me a palate that never seems to be satisfied, always thirsting for more. Without your guidance and life advice I don't know where I would have ended up. Thank you for being understanding of my crazy journey, and always being supportive, every step of the way.

To my dad: for being so talented at seemingly everything you do. I'm forever grateful to be the son of someone who can do, fix, and provide everything. Every day, I find myself doing a new task, starting a new hobby, finishing up an old project, and starting a new one. Your work ethic and ingenuity live within me and is one of the main reasons why I cook and live the way I do. Thank you for always pushing me to achieve my outlandish goals and helping me build my wild life.

To my sister: you pushed me to drop out of college and pursue a career in food, so you're the reason I began this journey 20+ years ago. And of course, for the three little boys who make me an uncle.

To my family: you're everything and I love you.

To my Messermeister family: you believed in me from the very beginning. By creating and collaborating on the Adventure Chef Collection years ago, we opened a portal to what would become my future. You ladies believed in me when very few others did. I am forever grateful for the life you've led me into, like older sisters, providing advice, mentoring me in business, and putting me on course for success.

To Tex: we were both lost puppies when we found each other in West Texas. I'm grateful to have you by my side.

And finally to Alexander Rigby: I'll never forget receiving that first email from Alex, a Senior Editor from DK/Penguin Random House. He wanted to work on a cookbook with me. My jaw dropped to the floor. In an instant, my dreams of writing a cookbook came true—and with the world's best publisher, nevertheless. Pinch me, I'm still dreaming. Thank you, Alex.

INDEX

ABOUT THE AUTHOR

ADAM GLICK has spent more than a decade sailing around the world as a private yacht chef. He's covered more than 100,000 nautical miles, visited 70+ countries, and accumulated stories for a lifetime. His travels and challenges while cooking professionally, combined with his passion for the outdoors, have primed him for a life of preparing five-star food in beautiful, remote, and off-grid locations. He has appeared on the television shows *Below Deck Mediterranean*, *Below Deck Sailing Yacht*, *Cutthroat Kitchen*, and *Stoked*.

The lifestyle Adam leads now is focused on minimalism, simplicity, and nature. He is happiest cooking with no kitchen at all, with the formalities of his previous life stripped away so he can focus on what matters most. Today, you can find Adam continuing his love for feeding people by embracing a more primal, methodic, and simple way of cooking. Residing in a cozy little cabin in the Pacific Northwest, Adam enjoys spending time with his dog, Tex, overlanding, cooking for friends and family, and continuing to create and inspire others to live free and eat well.

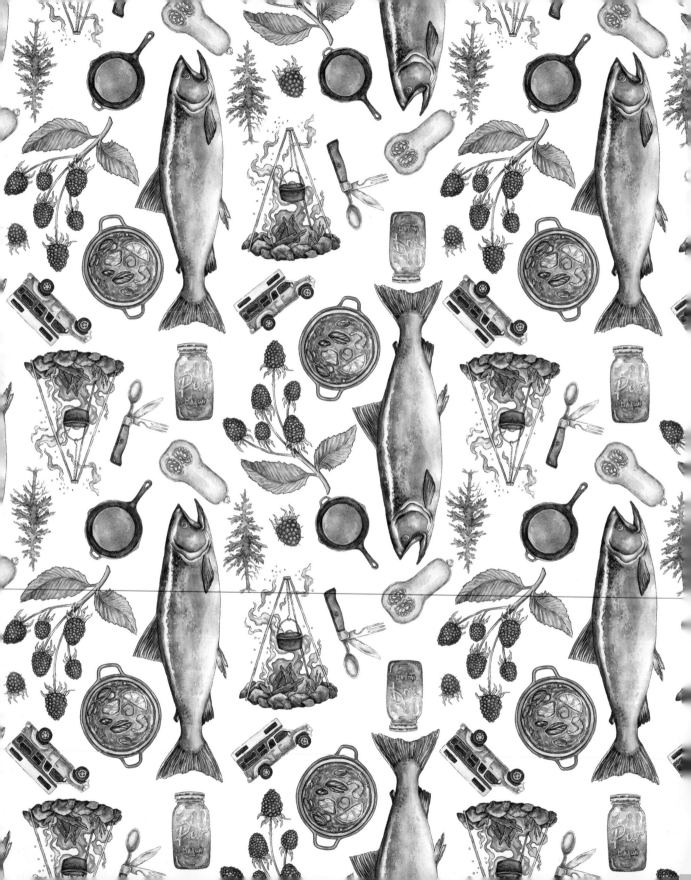